THE PERFECT
HOME
FOR A LONG
LIFE

CHOOSING THE RIGHT
RETIREMENT
LIFESTYLE FOR YOU

D1009136

THE PERFECT HOME FOR A LONG LIFE

CHOOSING THE RIGHT RETIREMENT LIFESTYLE FOR YOU

Lyndsay Green

THOMAS ALLEN PUBLISHERS   TORONTO

Library and Archives Canada Cataloguing in Publication

Green, Lyndsay
    The perfect home for a long life : choosing the right retirement lifestyle
for you / Lyndsay Green.

Includes index.
Issued also in electronic formats.
ISBN 978-1-77102-271-2

1. Older people—Housing. 2. Older people—Care. I. Title.

HD7287.9.G74   2013   363.5'946   C2012-908528-6

Editors: Katherine Ashenburg and Janice Zawerbny
Cover design: Sputnik Design Partners Inc.
Cover image: istock.com

Published by Thomas Allen Publishers,
a division of Thomas Allen & Son Limited,
390 Steelcase Road East,
Markham, Ontario L3R 1G2 Canada

www.thomasallen.ca

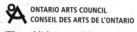

The publisher gratefully acknowledges the support of The Ontario Arts Council for its publishing program.

We acknowledge the support of the Canada Council for the Arts, which last year invested $20.1 million in writing and publishing throughout Canada.

We acknowledge the Government of Ontario through the Ontario Media Development Corporation's Ontario Book Initiative.

We acknowledge the financial support of the Government of Canada through the Canada Book Fund for our publishing activities.

13 14 15 16 17 5 4 3 2 1

Text printed on 100% PCW recycled stock

Printed and bound in Canada

To my parents with love and gratitude

Contents

What We Need from Our Home 39

Acknowledgments

This book has been enriched by the generosity of dozens of people who shared their stories about housing and life. My heartfelt thanks goes to Alison Acker, Jane Algire, Dorothy Ames, Sydney Bacon, Marjorie Bain, David Barnes, Bob Breadon, Beth Breadon, Lynda Clark, Tom Croil, Suzie Cunningham, Barb Emery, Dale Flexman, Gail Flitton, Eric Fowether, Sigi Franiek, Oli Franiek, Jean Garsonnin, Fred Gordon, Paula Granter, Michael Gregson, Dorothy Henaut, Gerald Hodge, Reva Horowitz, Hudson Janisch, Paul Jarsky, Ann Kirkland, Henry Kroll, Jean Kroll, Gloria Lattanzio, John Lawson, Sue Lawther, Gord Leidal, Peggy Lister, Tom Lownie, Bev Lownie, Ruth MacKenzie, Jenny Mansfield, Donna McCaw, Marcia McClung, Bob McMullen, Ruth Miller, Maureen Molaro, Anne Moon, Pat Morrow, Wanda O'Hagan, Maureen O'Neil, Joanna Patrick, Betty Pletcher, Judith Rinfret, Geraldine Sherman, Ricardo Smith, Bobbie Speck, Fred Spoke, Jim Sugiyama, Mary Sugiyama, Fran Thoburn, Joy Trimble, Betty Tudor, and Harry Tudor. The book has benefitted greatly from the expertise of the following people who reviewed the manuscript and shared their observations and insights: Jane Algire, Skip Bassford, Ann Carlyle, Jane Darville, Vince Gilpin, Alan Gratias, Marcia McClung, Suzanne Robinson, Russ Scorgie, Nancy Singer, Dr. Samir Sinha, and Cheryl Snider. My talented editors, Katherine Ashenburg and Janice Zawerbny, along with the terrific Thomas Allen team have tried to make the book as good as it could be, and made writing it a joy. A special thanks to my marketing genius, Andrea Intven. All things are possible thanks to the love and support of my family—Hank, Lauren, and Andrea, for whom I have daily reason to give thanks.

THE PERFECT
HOME
FOR A LONG
LIFE

**CHOOSING THE RIGHT
RETIREMENT
LIFESTYLE FOR YOU**

Introduction

WHEN boomers and seniors talk about the golden years, there is a refrain that concludes many of our conversations. After describing our hopes that we'll finally learn to play the piano or take that cruise around the world, or voicing our fears that we'll lose our marbles or outlive our money, we sum things up with a variation on this statement: "Whatever happens, there's no way I'm going to end up in a nursing home." Despite this pledge, most of us are probably not doing much to avoid this outcome. Some of us are confident we'll drop dead on the golf course or drift off in our sleep before we need institutional care. And the rest of us figure we've got decades of active living before we have to face this issue. But after canvassing the opinion of people already living in elderland, I have lost my confidence that a positive future will take care of itself. For the book *You Could Live a Long Time: Are You Ready?*, I asked 40 elders between the ages of 75 and 100 what boomers should be doing now to maximize our chances of living well, right to the end. They warned that if we don't take steps now to house ourselves for the future, others may end up making those decisions for us, and we may not be happy with the outcome. Their advice was pointed. We should modify our home to accommodate an aging mind and body. We should downsize and get rid of clutter. We should choose a neighbourhood that offers lots of stimulation and easy access to services. We should surround ourselves with a community of caring and loving people.

This advice from the elders makes eminent sense, but the devil is in the details. Often the choices are not clear-cut and the decisions can be difficult. There are countless factors to consider—finances, timing, our physical and cognitive limitations, the wishes of significant others in our lives—and then there's plain old inertia. And even if we were to get serious about delineating the ideal solution, the option we're looking for may not exist.

I wrote this book to provide concrete examples of the myriad ways that aging boomers and seniors are finding their communities and organizing their living arrangements to support lives of quality and fulfillment. The book looks at downsizing, modifying our home, and choosing retirement communities. As well, it considers innovative approaches such as homesharing, cohousing, supportive housing, and religious, ethnocultural, and spiritual communities. The focus is on practical solutions and replicable ideas with insights into the benefits and challenges of each option. You'll read about strategies to fit all budgets and levels of care needs. The choices are illuminated through interviews with people who are living the experience. To encourage complete candour, I promised the interviewees I would change their names and disguise their locations. This way, you'll find out what they really think.

This book is about creating a home for ourselves as we age, whether it be in a room, an apartment, a house, or a Tumbleweed House—which you'll read about later. The distinction between a home and a house is an important one, and acknowledges that we can make a home for ourselves in any manner of physical structure. In *Home: A Short History of an Idea*, Witold Rybczynski sums up the difference neatly: "You could walk out of the house, but you always returned home." He explains that the concept of *home* developed over time to bring together "the meanings of house and of household, of dwelling and of refuge, of ownership and of affection."[1]

When I started this exercise my goal was to use the findings for my own life. I wanted to figure out where and how I should live, with the objective of applying the elders' advice and supporting my active aging. But I learned that, instead of making one housing decision, I am more likely to face a series of choices as I respond to changing circumstances. I will probably have several old ages as I react to life's curve balls, whether medical issues, financial challenges, the loss of loved ones, or, on the positive side, opportunities for new adventures.

Also, I realized that we're going to have to stretch our imaginations. Many of the options in this book may not be available in our neighbourhood, so we may need to take the initiative and organize new services that will satisfy our future requirements. The happy outcome will be a solution for ourselves as well as improved choices for others. The stories in this book allow us to try on different modes of living and see how they fit. Even if a particular approach doesn't suit now, it could be one to keep in storage. If we find an option that really looks good, the book's links to resources and research findings will help us create the future we want.

Before exploring our alternatives, I want to lay out the hard facts that will affect our options. This will be followed by a look at some developments that will positively affect the future, and then a discussion about the characteristics we need in our home. After exploring the housing ideas, the book concludes with lessons learned—some overriding principles to guide us while we ponder our options and make those tough decisions.

When we're finding it difficult to motivate ourselves to tackle some nebulous housing needs in a remote future, it may help to remember the impetus for the elders I interviewed in *You Could Live a Long Time: Are You Ready?* What drove them to stay in control of their future was a desire to maintain their independence as long as possible, and a wish not to be a burden to others. And they wanted to be able to continue their lives of engagement, contribution, and personal growth—right to the end. Goals worth the effort.

Background

WHEN my parents were in their ninth decade, they were forced to leave their home of 34 years. It all began the day my mother was taken on a stretcher down the front steps of their house into a waiting ambulance. She would never see her home again. It had been a relatively minor accident—a collarbone broken in a fall. But after she had been treated, the medical staff assessed her living conditions and decided her home was unsuitable for her recovery. When she was moved to a long-term care facility, my father, who could no longer drive, spent hours transferring from bus to bus so that he could reach her distant location and spend time with her. Dad made this pilgrimage daily for weeks until we were able to persuade him to sell their house and move to a retirement residence located near Mom's facility. Five years later, they are together in an excellent long-term care residence, but the journey has been excruciatingly painful. After watching them, I felt compelled to figure out where I am going to live when I get old, because I am attempting to avoid their fate. I figured

that if this could happen to them, it could happen to anyone—including me.

My father had been a planner, a strategic thinker, and
a doer. He topped off his civil engineering degree with an
MBA from Harvard University and had a career as an operations manager in the oil industry. Dad believed in always
thinking three steps ahead. So I wasn't surprised when, at
the age of 80, he asked me to help him evaluate housing
options with the goal of moving my mother and him from
their home to smaller and more suitable accommodation.
I lived in a different city and didn't have a daily sense of
their changing needs, but I could tell that their physical and
mental health was diminishing. I was immensely relieved
and proud to see that Dad, in his usual fashion, was antici-
pating the problems and gearing into action. He recognized that their two-storey home was rife with land mines
for the elderly and knew the time had come to relocate to
greener and safer pastures. He asked me to help him exam-
ine their options, including downsizing to an apartment or
relocating to a retirement residence. Their choices were
virtually limitless, with many desirable options. They had
all the financial resources they needed and, at that point,
both of them were well enough and charming enough to be
welcomed everywhere.

Over a period of months we toured many facilities and
explored many neighbourhoods while Dad drew up extensive graphs comparing the options in terms of cost, size of
apartment, desirability of location, and amenities. The process seemed destined for success. What I failed to under-

stand was that while Dad's ability to make spreadsheets and evaluate options remained sharp, his decision-making capacity had departed. And although my mother was in on the discussions from the very beginning, and gave us her wish list for amenities and discussed our findings, for her it was an abstract exercise. She never intended to move.

When my parents initiated this process with me, I had no idea it would be half a decade before they were housed in a safe and supportive environment. And it was beyond my imagining to envision the three-page chronology that those years would provide: of plans unrealized, contracts cancelled, and opportunities not seized. The result was anxiety and anguish for many in our family, but particularly for my parents. That outcome we boomers fear was also my parents' dread, and it was to be their fate. They will end their lives having spent many years in what they would have called a nursing home.

I learned a great deal from my parents' experience and have interwoven the lessons through this book. But I'll save the biggest finding for the end. You see, my parents had a backup plan and it was that plan that saved them from complete disaster. So, once you've read about all the housing options and considered the guiding principles, I'll suggest one last thing for you to put in place. Let's call it Plan B. But first let's look at Plan A—housing ourselves with an eye to the future.

What We Want

I F I ASKED each of us to envision a home for our later years, we would probably agree on some general objectives. We want to live in a home that supports our independence, in a place with opportunities for fellowship and engagement. Beyond that, the specifics would vary greatly. Some want to live out their lives in the city, town, or neighbourhood where they currently reside. For them, the streets and buildings are infused with memories that enrich their days and they couldn't imagine abandoning their personal history. Relocating would mean moving away from family, friends, former work colleagues—or a beloved hairdresser, doctor, or fitness instructor. And if they intend to keep working, moving might mean leaving behind their business or clients. To achieve the goal of staying put, they'll need to reconfigure their home to anticipate long-term needs, or identify suitable accommodation nearby.

Others are ready for a move and are prepared to put down roots somewhere completely new. They may be drawn to places that are physically beautiful or have a more desirable climate. They may be seeking a location that better supports their interests and activities, whether boating, hiking, farming, skiing, golfing, gardening, academic studies, or the arts. Some want to move closer to family or friends, or return to a place where they spent their childhood. Others want to live full time in a vacation home. Some may simply want the brain-stretching exercise that comes with making one's way in new terrain.

Some are keen to have new adventures in their later years, maybe necessitating unconventional living arrangements. They may want to travel and take their home with them, in a backpack, on a boat, or in an RV. They may decide to sell their home in order to free up capital to pursue other passions. They may want to split their time among several locations to seize opportunities that would let them perfect their language skills, practise their sport, or have several chances to see flowers bloom in spring.

But while we are organizing to achieve our immediate goals, it is to our advantage to incorporate planning for the very long term. Assuming we live long enough, most of us will outlive our current mental or physical capacity, and pretty well all of us will need some assistance for daily living.

Budget considerations play into our decisions. Can I afford to continue living where I am? What will it cost to modify my home versus buying something ready-made? Does it make more sense to rent or buy? Can I afford to live in the location of my dreams? If I want to continue to work, will that be possible living here? Can I afford the travel costs associated with my dream location, whether they involve driving to see family or flying to holiday destinations? Do health or financial circumstances require me to co-locate with family or friends?

These decisions are further complicated because we rarely make them alone. Our family and friends may be weighing in strongly with their opinions on what we should do. We may be planning a future jointly with a spouse or partner. We may have care responsibilities for others and their needs must be taken into account. And then there are the unexpected developments that can restructure our priorities and throw previous plans out the window, whether sad ones such as a death or an illness in the family, or happy ones such as the arrival of grandchildren or a commitment to a new partner.

Underlying our decisions are some fine lines we're trying to walk. One critical balance point lies between our independence and our need for community. Most of us want to inhabit a physical space where we are in charge, where we make the rules about how things run, what items will decorate our surroundings, what time we'll have dinner, what music will be playing, whether we'll leave our bed unmade today. On the flip side, we are social creatures and our need for care, companionship, affection, admiration, and validation is always present and, in some cases, increases with age. Having both independence and community requires compromise, and those of us who live with others understand that fine line and walk it daily. Every housing option will require us to give up some privacy and some self-reliance in order to support our independence as we age.

Another fine line lies between safety and security versus risk-taking. Our need to be surrounded by the familiar and predictable often increases with age, yet to stay vital we need to keep pushing ourselves and trying new things. We need novelty to continue to grow, and if things are too safe we get bored and lose our appetite for life. If we set ourselves up so securely that old patterns never have to be modified and life offers no surprises, we may feel as though we're merely marking time until the end. Our housing choice will place us somewhere on that spectrum. Let's take stairs, for example. Because they force us to exercise, we shouldn't give them up too soon. Maybe we can extend their safety with better handrails, good-grip flooring, and improved lighting. But if we lose our mobility, those same stairs become an impassable barrier and reduce our options. Similarly, if we move into an environment where others take over our responsibilities, whether cooking, gardening, or managing our investments, we may lose vital stimulation and sense of purpose. But if we reach a point where we start forgetting to turn off the stove, can no longer bend down to weed, or lose our financial acumen, we'll need to accept help. Ideally, our environment will be as stimulating as we can handle and, when we require more safety, security, and familiarity, we will be able to adjust our surroundings accordingly.

The Hard Facts

Our Home Can Make or Break Us

FOR SENIORS, not all homes are created equal and, in many ways, our homes can make or break us as we age. Falls account for 85 per cent of seniors' injury-related hospitalizations, and falls are the cause of most hip fractures among seniors. Half of the falls resulting in hospitalization occur in or around the home. I remember when my grandmother, then in her mid-seventies, fell and broke her hip. I was horrified at the grim predictions from her friends that this accident signalled "game over" for her. Happily, she recovered and had another decade and a half of mainly good health. Although her friends were wrong in her case, their dire prognosis had a factual basis. The Public Health Agency of Canada reports that half of the seniors who break a hip never recover full functioning, and one in five will die within 12 months of suffering the fracture. When these accidents happen at home, it might not have been their home that killed them, but it was probably an accomplice.[1]

When a lot of elderly people die at once, it's even easier to see just how dangerous it can be to live in your own home. During the August 2003 heat wave in France, nearly 15,000 people were killed. Many of the deceased were elderly and most of them were living in their own homes. Research published in the *European Journal of Public Health* found that lack of mobility was a major risk factor along with some pre-existing medical conditions, but the buildings themselves were a factor in the deaths. You were at greatest risk of death if you were living in an old building without thermal insulation, if your bedroom was located directly under the roof, if you were confined to bed, and had a cardiovascular or neurological disease or mental disorder. And you were more vulnerable if you lived in a building without greenery to moderate the extreme temperature buildup.[2]

The potential for our home to turn on us is illustrated well by the story Liz tells. She decided that she and her partner had to leave their 16-acre rural property before it killed them or their guests. "Our realization that we were going to have to sell came gradually," she explains. "Since our place was at the bottom of a hill, every time there was a storm we could be cut off for a couple of days. You hear stories and start to worry. What if someone has a medical problem and the snowplow hasn't come to clear our long steep lane? Then a friend who was with us for New Year's Eve had what appeared to be a heart attack and we realized we'd have to call a helicopter to get him to the hospital in time. Fortunately he revived and recovered on his own. Then there was the time we got into the car to drive to a party and the fog started to close in and we couldn't see five feet in front of us. Shortly after that a friend of ours fell asleep at the wheel and drove off the road and nearly killed herself. Then my partner began to injure himself, and this had always been a big worry because he has inherited brittle bones. His arm turned black after lifting rocks in the garden. And then he slipped in his bedroom slippers and hurt his back. From then on, he was always in a lot of pain and it just got too hard physically. We could have simply let the property deteriorate, but I wouldn't have been able to bear that from an aesthetic point of view. And there is the investment to consider. Our place would only hold its property value while it had all those things people want—paddocks, pond, pastures—that beautiful tranquillity you sense coming down the hill. But it all takes work. If we had been extremely wealthy we could have hired help—but we weren't. So after I turned 60, we sold the property and moved into a much lower-maintenance property in a village."

The recent shift in government policy away from institutional care toward supporting elderly people to live independently in their own homes has made the potentially lethal nature of our housing particularly significant. This "aging in place" strategy is touted as both the right thing for seniors as well as the most economical approach for government. As an example, the 2012 Ontario provincial budget proposed a number of measures to support seniors in their homes because "it costs taxpayers more to provide seniors' care in a long-term care home than it does to support seniors who live in their own home or with a family member." The measures included expanding house calls, increasing access to home care, and providing improved care coordination.[3]

This governmental resolve to have us age in place sounds good to many of us who are determined to stay at home until the very end. But we're probably envisioning an end that is quick, preceded by a fully capable and vigorous life. More predictably, we'll be like my parents and live a good number of years with decreasing abilities. If this decline is going to happen at home, we had better take a good hard look at our surroundings. And it's not just the physical space that should concern us, it's how we will get the psychic nurturing and emotional support we will need. Without the appropriate home environment and adequate care support, our idyllic vision of aging in place could turn into a nightmare. One crucial factor that will affect this future will be our financial resources, which is the next hard fact.

Financial Constraints May Require Compromises/Creativity

Some financial analysts recommend that we plan for retirement by budgeting for 60 or 70 per cent of our pre-retirement income, while others warn that to maintain our lifestyle, we'll need to keep our income at pre-retirement levels. It looks as though it's going to be particularly hard for retired middle-income boomers to maintain their income. The Institute for Research on Public Policy calculates that approximately one-half of Canadians who were born between 1945 and

1970 and have average annual earnings of between $35,000 and $80,000 are likely to experience a drop in income of at least 25 per cent once they reach retirement.[4]

Those with limited means find that aging brings even more strains to already challenging living situations. The Older Women's Network (OWN) has been sounding the alarm bells for decades. When the non-profit organization was founded in 1986, one of its first actions was to hold a public forum on housing "to address the severe housing problems of older women." Since then, OWN has advocated for suitable affordable housing by conducting research, making submissions to government bodies, and holding public events. The report from their 2009 forum, "Options and Priorities for Affordable Housing," sets out some hard-hitting facts. According to 2006 Statistics Canada data, the percentage of women 65 and over who are poor is almost double that of men (8.7 per cent of women, versus 4.4 per cent of men.) Aging women are especially affected by the lack of affordable housing because they live longer than men, have lower incomes when in the workforce, and have fewer benefits when they retire since they often take time from their career to care for children and elders. As well, senior women are more likely to be unattached and, if you're unattached, there's a greater likelihood that you'll be poor.[5]

OWN has been developing its own strategies for responding to the need. Back in 1997, they developed the OWN Housing Co-op, a 142-unit building in Toronto. The co-op has a mixed-income population, mostly mid-life or older woman and men, along with some families and young people, and about three-quarters of residents benefit from subsidized rent.[6] Recently, OWN launched the lecture series "What Really Works in Creating Affordable Housing," and they conduct tours of buildings and projects that feature affordable housing solutions. These activities explore many of the topics discussed in this book, including life lease projects, cohousing, initiatives by charitable and community organizations to develop senior housing, and low-cost rental and ownership options.[7]

As we move forward, each of us will need a financial plan that anticipates our housing needs. For example, if we want to age in place, we'll need to budget for the operating and maintenance of our living space, as well as for home care costs to support our daily needs. Since some of us won't have as much money as we'd like, we'll have to get creative to achieve our goals. Many options in this book reflect this reality, whether sharing accommodation expenses, using our home as an income generator, or finding or developing affordable seniors housing. As you'll read, some of these strategies require innovative approaches to living space, and a few compromises.

We May Develop Physical and Cognitive Disabilities

If we're lucky to live long enough, there's a good chance we'll develop a disability. My friend Bonnie had a stroke just before she turned 50 and now needs to use a mobility device. She reminds me gently that I am "temporarily able-bodied." According to the Canadian government's 2011 Federal Disability Report, about 43 per cent of seniors report having a disability. The most commonly reported disabilities relate to mobility, agility, and pain, while the less frequently reported relate to hearing, seeing, memory, communication, learning, and emotional disabilities. The older you get, the greater your chances of developing disabilities, and, often, multiple disabilities. Nearly three-quarters of people aged 85 and older report disabilities, and over half of them have more than four disabilities.[8] All disabilities are not created equal, nor are they perceived in the same way, and the report acknowledges the role played by beliefs and attitudes in the way disabilities are acknowledged and handled. While some problems can be treated as a natural part of aging, others are too debilitating to be dealt with by a sunny disposition. Fifty-eight per cent of seniors aged 85 and over report having severe to very severe disabilities.

Many of us who develop disabilities will be able to live independently as long as we have access to support and are willing to utilize it. The elders whose wisdom was summarized in *You Could Live a Long Time: Are You Ready?* emphasized that to stay independent as we age, we'll need to learn to accept help, and many of the options explored in this book include support that might eliminate, or at least delay, a move to institutional care.

We'll Likely Outlive Our Driver's Licence

Despite the most fervent hope of many of us, we may not be able to continue driving until our dying days. One report estimates that seniors on average will live at least 7 to 10 years beyond their ability to drive.[9] Although research has put to rest the stereotype that an older driver is automatically an unsafe driver, many of us choose to restrict our driving as we age.[10] We might confine it to local streets and avoid freeways and we may avoid night driving. At age 80, Betsy just got her licence renewed but decided to sell her car. "I'll use public transit or walk," she explains, "and if I really need a car I'll rent or use AutoShare by-the-hour rentals."

It was the issue of driving that made Harriet and her husband rethink their retirement plans. "We used to have a farm where we spent weekends and holidays," Harriet explains, "and we always thought we would build our retirement home there. But a major problem developed with this concept—my husband and I began to hate cars. And you can't live in the country without a car. It would have been completely impractical. The other problem with our dream of rural living is that if one of you develops health problems, you're really in trouble. So when we turned 65, we sold the farm instead of retiring to it."

Harriet and her husband are now in their early seventies and gave up their car a couple of years ago. "We live downtown and can walk or bike everywhere," she says, "so we haven't missed driving. This is one step toward accepting getting old that we have taken. My mother was still driving at 91 and not only was she driving herself around, she was also driving her friends. It terrified me. Her arthritis was very bad and she was well beyond the point at which she should have given up her licence. So when she finally said, 'I think I'm going to have to sell the car,' we had it sold in two days. Our retirement plans do not include a car."

Despite the impracticalities and the dangers, many of us want to keep driving because it fulfills needs that go way beyond transportation. In her memoir *Somewhere Towards the End*, Diana Athill captures our complicated love affair with the car. At age 88, her legs have almost given out and she finds it difficult and painful to walk even a hundred yards. At this point her car begins to represent life. "You hobble towards it, you ease your unwieldy body laboriously into the driver's seat—and lo! you are back to normal. Off you whizz just like everyone else, restored to freedom, restored (almost) to youth. I always liked my car. Now I love it." But she acknowledges that this increased love and dependence has coincided with the deterioration of other things besides her legs, and she describes several accidents she was in, one caused by "being an overtired *old person* flustered by her own silliness in landing herself in an awkward situation."[11]

No doubt we boomers will successfully lobby to have elder drivers' ability more accurately and fairly assessed, which should mean that safe drivers can stay on the road longer. But it would still be wise for us to plan for a car-free existence. This means living somewhere with good transportation services, and amenities within walking distance or in range for a motorized scooter. If the public transit system is inadequate we'll need to rely on some version of the ride service offered through service groups discussed in the upcoming section on community support. We may also consider carpooling, an option that is growing in popularity thanks to services such as eRideShare.com. This service offers personal matchups for regular or one-off trips, and there are postings for many Canadian locations from both drivers and passengers looking to share expenses. The *New York Times* reports that another ride-sharing website, Ridejoy, plans to introduce digital identification verification and background checks to their service to reassure people who like the concept of sharing rides but have safety concerns.[12]

Kathy and her husband gave up their car when she was 65 and her husband was 75, and she has these tips for liberating yourself from your vehicle. "Imagine your life without a car so that when it happens you won't feel your life is coming to an end. Choose your activities and friends with a mind to the fact that you aren't going to be driving. Be kind to young friends so you can ask them to pick you up. We are so car-fixated. Give up the keys."

Moving Only Gets More Difficult

Moving does not get easier by putting it off. The longer we wait, the harder it gets. I learned this watching my parents agonize over downsizing from their home. My parents knew they needed to get into a more supportive environment, and it was at their initiative that I helped them explore the options. Yet they backed away from one planned relocation a year over a five-year period. First, they cancelled the purchase of a beautiful nearby condo after the deal was virtually signed. My father's explanation for their decision to renege had some logic: "We'll only have to move again at some point into more assisted living." After that, they signed agreements and then backed away from a succession of high-end retirement residences. Each time the option was highly desirable: a vibrant location, good food, independent living with supportive dining and recreation options at their discretion. A middle-aged friend who was watching the process said, "I would move into any one of these places right now—if I could afford it." When push came to shove, they couldn't do it, and we couldn't make them, and it was only that medical emergency that pushed them out the door.

Whether you're going to modify your home or downsize, it's going to get harder over time. Moving is physically demanding, mentally challenging, and emotionally draining. As we age we usually find ourselves with less energy and a diminished ability to face the ruptures of renovation or packing or relocation, and inertia sets in. After a certain point, only a catastrophe will propel change. The rule of thumb seems to be that if you haven't downsized from the family home by the time you're in your eighties, it's unlikely to happen. Many people make a move after that age but most of them have already reduced their living space and are moving again to more assisted living.

One of the greatest barriers to downsizing is our fear of dealing with the accumulated possessions of a lifetime. Lucille and her husband, Stan, are both 85 and have been living in their home for 54 years. They say they want to move while they can still retain control of the decision-making over their future. But Lucille dreads the thought of "dealing with all the stuff." "Every drawer I open I think, 'Who would want this?'" she asks, wincing. "If you get someone to help you, there's the embarrassment of explaining to them why you kept these things all these years. Like the vase I've hung on to for decades because of the memory it evokes of a deceased relative. I heard recently about the idea of taking a photo of things like my vase, which are imbued with memories. Then I could give away the vase and keep the photo. That's really all I need."

Lucille has a powerful incentive to tackle this challenge because of her health issues, but even so, she hasn't done anything yet and her reluctance is palpable. "I know I need to face this soon because my legs aren't getting any better," she explains. "We need to be on one floor with no stairways, but I really dread the thought."

Harriet says that her parents' pain was eased by giving them a year to come to terms with the move before the deed was done. Harriet's mother was 84 and her father 85 when they admitted they were going to need much more support. They were living in a condo and getting help a couple of times a week, but they were struggling. Her father had developed Parkinson's and her mother had very bad arthritis. "I'm the eldest of five," Harriet explains, "and I gathered as many of my siblings as I could and we sat our parents down and said, 'What do you want to do?' We proposed that someone live with them full time and they said, 'Absolutely not.' They could see the wisdom of moving. They wanted to be somewhere where they could enjoy the company of other people when they wanted and then be able to go back to their own room and shut the door. They were prepared to move to a retirement home but asked for one more year in the condo to give themselves time to come to terms with the change. So we agreed to get them the additional help they would need to stay put for another year. When the time came, they moved into a large-sized suite in a residence that they loved. My mother is still there at 95 and my father was able to stay there for three years until his dementia reached the stage where he had to be moved to a long-term care facility. He died a few months later. Looking back, I realize how lucky we were that my parents handled things the way they did."

Reasons for Optimism

AFTER FACING the hard facts, we need to acknowledge the optimistic side of the ledger. Innovations in technology are converging with the creativity and energy of the growing senior cohort to expand our housing options. While this book explores the leading edge of current housing options, future developments will extend these horizons even farther and allow us to house ourselves in ways that would not have been feasible for previous generations. Here are some of the reasons for optimism.

The Demographic Shift

We're living longer, and the seniors of today are in better physical and mental health than our predecessors. Statistics Canada predicts that by 2031 one in four Canadians will be over 65. Products and services are being developed that cater to our growing and demanding cohort, especially in the cities and towns where we predominate. Being part of a pushy, large consumer group with high expectations and the time and expertise to turn aspirations into reality will change the aging landscape.

To get a sense of what a world designed for seniors of the future might look like, it's inspiring to watch developments in New York City. In 2009, the city released Age Friendly NYC, a blueprint for enhancing livability for its seniors, whose numbers are expected to increase by nearly 50 per cent over the next 20 years and who, for the first time, will outnumber school-age children. The plan, based on consultation with older New Yorkers, as well as academic, private, and non-profit sectors, outlines 59 specific initiatives focused on four areas: community and civic participation, housing, public spaces and transportation, and health and social services. In spring 2011, the city and the New York Academy of Medicine issued a progress report on these initiatives that makes for rousing reading.[1] Here are some of the highlights.

Hundreds of older adults and others have embraced the concept of "neighbors helping neighbors" by offering services through TimeBanksNYC, a program that lets New Yorkers volunteer their time and services in exchange for credits that can be redeemed for services. Examples include a professional craft designer teaching a crochet class for the Manhattan Valley Golden Age Senior Center, an older New Yorker who enjoys researching herbs and nutrition sharing this information with other older adults, and a professional artist teaching drawing classes. Yellow school buses, which previously sat idle during the school day, are being used to take older adults grocery shopping. Now older New Yorkers and others who rely on the Access-A-Ride paratransit service can use debit cards to take taxis, an option that is more time- and cost-efficient. A Silver Alert system helps New Yorkers assist the New York City Police Department in finding vulnerable older adults with cognitive impairments. Safe Streets for Seniors engaged older adults and community residents in surveying dangerous intersections. Improvements made in five pilot areas include modifying pedestrian signals to accommodate slower walking speeds, upgrading street markings for better visibility, installing pedestrian refuge islands, extending curbs to shorten crossing distances, and calming traffic through techniques such as lane reductions. And a campaign has been launched to fight hunger among seniors, including the Green Carts initiative, which has licensed vendors to sell fruits and vegetables in neighbourhoods where fresh produce is hard to obtain.

As part of a 2011 pilot program, New York City launched senior centres in eight locations that feature underwater photography courses, organic and vegetarian meals, rooftop gardening, swimming, technology courses, and video conferencing. The centres are free and open to people 60 and older, and include a site serving the lesbian, gay, bisexual, and transgender (LGBT) communities, as well as one for seniors with vision problems. Innovative approaches include offering studio space to artists in exchange for teaching art to senior centre members.[2] One of the projects in this Space for Art initiative was a documentary of seniors telling their life stories.

At New York's Mount Sinai Hospital, the growing number of older patients, coupled with the recognition that senior-friendly design can improve health outcomes, has led to the creation of an emergency room for people over 65. Features include skid-proof floors and extra handrails to help prevent falls, dimmable lighting and diurnal skylights that mimic natural outdoor lighting throughout the day, and curtains designed to muffle noise. There are extra heating units to keep older patients warm, special mattresses to help prevent bedsores, and lounge chairs designed to make it easier for geriatric patients to get in and out. Some rooms have tablet computers to allow patients to contact the nursing station.[3] In June 2010, New York was recognized by the World Health Organization (WHO) as the first municipality in the world to meet the WHO's criteria for an age-friendly city. Mayor Michael Bloomberg, born in 1942, says, "As an older New Yorker myself, I can proudly say that I have a personal, vested interest in building an age-friendly New York."

In Toronto, Mount Sinai Hospital is acknowledging the same incentive to respond more effectively to a growing senior patient base by introducing a hospital-wide geriatrics education program. Every single hospital staff member participates in an education program to raise his or her *geriatric awareness*. At the next level of contact, all clinical staff is being educated to increase their *geriatric knowledge*. According to Dr. Samir Sinha, director of Geriatrics, the goal is to "hardwire" geriatric knowledge and sensitivity into all aspects of the hospital's functioning to create an environment that is elder-friendly at every level.

Retirees Applying Their Expertise and Energy

We'll want to live in places with innovative senior-focused programs and services, but these developments don't just miraculously appear. Activists, many of whom are retirees, are changing the landscape for seniors by improving our housing options and redesigning our communities to make them more senior-friendly. Although every generation has paid some attention to the needs of the elderly, what's different this time is that more seniors are actively involved in the strategic thinking and program implementation. And we're acting with alacrity given our self-interest. The following examples from Brantford, Ontario, and Whistler, British Columbia, illustrate the positive impact that senior activists are having on our future choices.

Brantford, Ontario, has a master aging plan thanks to the initiative, knowledge, and commitment of two retired professionals: Lucy Marco, a businesswoman with decades of experience in health care, and Jean Kincade, an academic with graduate degrees in nursing and sociology. To improve the conditions for seniors in their community of about 94,000, the two activists pulled together a steering committee, galvanized local support, and raised funds to hire a facilitator to consult with the community. Their research found that priority issues for residents over 55 were transportation and housing that was affordable and suitable for seniors' needs. The findings were combined with community consultation to develop a master plan—a strategic road map for a comprehensive, coordinated set of community services for seniors. The Grand River Council on Aging was set up to oversee the plan's implementation, with a board that includes six seniors and six members from local agencies that provide services to seniors. The decision was taken to set up an independent organization because many seniors' issues (such as providing an integrated, county-wide transportation system) involve the cooperation of public, private, and government agencies and organizations, and the council has been able to bring together diverse groups who normally don't communicate with each other. This "made-in-Brantford master aging plan" has captured national interest, and the council has shared its expertise with other municipalities through webinars and consulting support.[4]

In Whistler, British Columbia, the dedication of people such as Sue Lawther and Gord Leidal is turning this resort municipality of 9,000 into a place that sustains and supports its seniors. Gord is a consulting engineer with a background in development. In 1996, when he was 58 years of age, he moved to Whistler to semi-retire. A year earlier, an organization called the Mature Action Committee (MAC) had been incorporated with the goal of improving housing options for Whistler seniors. Gord became president of MAC and realized they needed to kick-start the process. "We were trying to educate people about the need to provide seniors housing, not only to target lower-income seniors, but to expand the choices for everyone. But we were having difficulty and I knew we had to make an impact. So we raised money among ourselves to hire a planning consultant who did a needs survey that was focused on housing and the interests of the residents." Years later, these initial steps have resulted in the development of 24 senior housing units, with more in the planning stage.

Sue Lawther, the current president of MAC, moved full time to Whistler in 1994 when she and her husband had an opportunity to buy a local company. Previously, they had been weekenders trying to figure out a way to become permanent residents. After they retired, they were able to buy into MAC's first senior housing complex. "I see my involvement with MAC as a payback for this opportunity to buy affordable housing and my way of saying thank you for being able to continue to live in my community," she says. Sue has championed the expansion of MAC's mandate beyond housing with the goal of making Whistler a model community for aging in place. "We're using the World Health Organization's model for age-friendly cities," Sue explains, "and launching seniors programming for mind, body, and soul, including exercise programs, intergenerational programs with high-school students, needs assessment regarding transportation, and the beginnings of a seniors centre."[5] You'll read more about MAC's work, including tips from Gord and Sue about lessons learned, in the section Seniors Housing.

New Technology

Technical advancements have already changed our relationship with aging and, in the decades to come, the developments will be truly transformative. Currently, many seniors are able to remain in their own homes with the support of an emergency call system, or lifeline, that alerts loved ones or caregivers in case of an emergency. The future will see the expansion of this monitoring capacity to our entire home, which can be wired with intelligent systems to safeguard our health and provide us with automated reminders of our daily tasks. We'll be better able to self-monitor conditions such as diabetes and vital signs including pulse, blood pressure, and oxygen saturation. Wireless activity sensors can monitor our daily living patterns, detect variations, and send out daily e-mail summaries and emergency alerts to designated recipients. Our remote caregivers will know if we got out of bed in the morning, took our pills, or prepared our meals. We'll be able to use technology with even more ease than we do today to order our groceries, take classes, shop, and connect with family and friends.

Electronic cognitive aids will help us remember names, faces, and appointments, and find things such as glasses, wallets, and keys. Already we use our smartphones for many of these tasks, and the Internet search function has allowed us to outsource a good portion of our memory bank. As Nora Ephron wrote in *I Remember Nothing*, "The Senior Moment has become the Google moment, and it has a much nicer, hipper, younger, more contemporary sound, doesn't it? By handling the obligations of the search mechanism, you almost prove you can keep up."[6]

Some technological tools will ask us to accept a certain level of surveillance and personal data collection, and, if this means maintaining our independence, many of us will be prepared to give up some privacy. This is the case for Dorothy Rutherford who, at age 86, is participating in a project run by the Oregon Center for Aging and Technology (ORCATECH) in Portland, Oregon. Sensors have been installed throughout Dorothy's apartment to monitor the speed and frequency of her activities in order to collect data that may indicate health changes long before her quality of life is affected. When interviewed by the *New York Times*, Dorothy said, "I have no worries about privacy whatsoever. They are just sensors, not video cameras." The project also includes a wireless smart pillbox to remind her to take her daily vitamins, and a robot, nicknamed Celia, equipped with a video screen. Dorothy's granddaughter and great-granddaughter can remotely wheel Celia from room to room and operate the robot for a video chat.[7]

A version of the wired home is operational in Lincoln County, Maine, where a project called the Maine Approach uses technology to help dozens of people between the ages of 80 to 104 stay in their own homes. Project members choose from a menu of technological supports that includes webcams for video monitoring and sensors for door, motion, temperature, and water-leak detection. The pan-and-tilt cameras are password protected and accessible to authorized family and staff. Video spot checks are performed on schedule or when there is cause for concern, and the video snapshots are time-stamped. The room that is primarily monitored is the kitchen. The cameras have privacy buttons and can be covered with a napkin for immediate privacy. Dr. Allan Teel, founder of the Maine Approach, says, "Most members do not find these video spot checks an invasion of privacy. As a matter of fact, many members find great comfort in knowing someone is looking out for them."[8] Teel points out that for many, this approach is less intrusive than the daily presence of caregivers. The costs, which include technological support as one tool in a broader program, average $400 per month. As Teel says, this is "a small fraction of what they would expect to pay in an assisted-living facility or a nursing home." The big bonus, Teel adds, is that his members are "healthier and happier" in their own homes.[9] You'll read more about the Maine Approach in Community Support.

If you want to play with the future, go to the website of The Toronto Rehabilitation Institute (www.torontorehab.com), click on the Innovations Gallery, and spend some time with their interactive demos. The institute is developing technology to help the elderly age in place, and here you'll see some of their current projects. They include the use of a home detection system that uses a mask to monitor sleep apnea, a talking toilet that reminds people with dementia to wash their hands, a fall-detection system that uses a ceiling-mounted video camera to activate a voice-recognition system and call an emergency contact, and an anti-collision wheelchair that uses proximity sensor systems and user prompts to avoid accidents. Other projects in development include a Wayfinding Belt that uses a combination of GPS and Bluetooth technology to help you navigate your way outside by guiding you in the right direction, footwear insoles that tell you when you're losing balance through heightened foot sensation, and a lift system that makes it easier for caregivers to move patients at home.

Although these innovations may sound like the stuff of science fiction, some will become a standard part of our future. Undoubtedly, technological advances will reduce our need for institutionalization and help us age in place, but they will never replace our need for human touch. To live fully as we age, we'll need much more than wires and gadgets.

What We Need from Our Home

OUR CHOICE of housing, both its physical features and location, is going to determine whether we'll have a safe, supportive, and life-affirming environment as we age. This section looks at what we need from our home. It's a tall order.

Allows Us to Stay Engaged

To be happy in our old age we will need a sense of engagement, and where we live will be a factor in whether we can find that "deep connection to something positive, meaningful, invigorating, and inspiring." This is the definition of engagement that Boston's Sloan Center on Aging & Work used for its research on the link between well-being and engagement, and they found that we have a deeper sense of well-being when we are highly engaged (not just involved) in activities. They say that to be engaged in an activity or role is "to be able to embrace it physically, cognitively, and emotionally." What results is a state of mind characterized by "vigour, dedication, and absorption." The research found that in later life the depth of engagement is even more consequential for well-being than in our earlier years.[1]

Phil exemplifies the Sloan Center research findings, and his location in a small community of about a thousand creative, energetic people has let him relish his lifelong passion for music. The community recently set up a radio station that is volunteer-operated and financed, and offers 16 hours of programming daily. Every Sunday afternoon, Phil hosts a jazz program. At 80 years of age, he's sharing his prodigious knowledge and extensive music collection with a broader audience. "I get quite 'high' doing this program," he says. "Jazz is one of the loves of my life. I've been a fan and a collector since I was 15 years old, and doing this show takes me back to my university days when I had a program at the campus radio station." Phil points to a bus parked next to his house and says, "I've kept every one of my records since I was a kid and they're all out there. I bought the dentist's bus when he got a new one and it's full of built-in cupboards and drawers that I use for my record collection. I have a beautiful velvet wingback chair and ottoman, and that's where I sit to listen to my music."

Moving closer to the centre of her city of about 350,000 people gave Irma an outlet for her passion for civic engagement. After relocating three years ago, at age 79, she began working with the homeless. "I take the minutes at the meetings for the street people for the Committee to End Homelessness," she explains. "The street people call me 'crack granny'! My work with the homeless keeps my small problems in proper focus. The difficulty with some seniors is they say 'I'm a crone and I'm here to give you my wisdom,' rather than being prepared to learn from young people. We need more bridging opportunities to give seniors a soft entrance into volunteering. You don't want to be overwhelmed, and when you get older you spend a lot of time on self-service, but it's really important to be part of your community."

Other people select their location for its potential to provide engagement through an encore career. Nigel is 61, and he and his partner, Rick, have been together for 18 years. About a decade ago they moved to a small town of about five thousand people that is a tourist mecca for arts and culture and opened a gift shop. They bought a heritage building and moved the store into the ground floor. The building includes an apartment on the top floor where they could move when they want to downsize from their home. But this is not a consideration for the immediate future. "There's no talk of retirement," Rick says. "Psychologically we're talking about ramping up!" They are delighted with the opportunities this new business affords them to live their dream lifestyle. "We travel to Europe twice a year and spend weeks purchasing the gifts and accessories we offer in our store—and the rest of the time we live in this charming spot." One of the side benefits of the store has been the way it connects them with kindred spirits. "Our store attracts people with similar tastes and interests to ours," Nigel explains, "so it's been a good way of identifying like-minded people who then become friends."

Gwen retired at age 55 and now, at 70, says, "It was stupid to give up my job as early as I did." As soon as she stopped working she missed both the income and the contact with young people. She moved to a new city and was grateful that her new location provided opportunities for part-time work. "I like having young friends," she says, "and when you're out of the workforce and you're old, they're hard to meet. So, ever since I moved here, I've done part-time work. I've done a range of things—worked in a doctor's office, did research for a pollster. Also, I do quite a bit of house-sitting and, although I don't get paid much, it lowers my costs of living because I can turn everything off in my rental apartment. I really have to watch my expenses because my rent has been going up."

In the above examples it was the location that provided the capacity for engagement, but paying attention to the physical layout of your home can ensure that you can support your activities. Can you carve out the space you need for an office, or a workshop, or an artist's studio? And if you're living with a partner or roommate, you'll need to multiply the workspace by two. From watching her father age, Glenda learned the importance of engagement as well as the importance of a self-contained workshop. "All winter Dad would work away at his carpentry," she remembers. "He made birdhouses and toys, which he gave away. He had his own space where he could disappear and make all the noise he wanted and apply his own standards of neatness."

Has Proximity to Our Emotional Circle

The elders whose wisdom was summarized in *You Could Live a Long Time: Are You Ready?* encouraged us to develop the richest possible social network of friends and family because we'll need to draw on these resources as we age. I call this our RECP (Retirement Emotional Circle Plan) and it's clear we should be giving this as much weight in our retirement plans as our RRSP (Registered Retirement Savings Plan). Some people will choose to live in proximity to a long-standing emotional circle of support, one that has been part of their lives for decades. Those who opt to relocate will want to select a place with a high potential for cultivating friendships and creating intimacies. If you're moving with a partner, he or she can help ease the transition, but if you're unattached you'll need a strong potential network. Most of us will have a combination of old and new friends in our emotional circle as we age, and some of them will play more significant roles than others. As well, it is likely that people will be paid to be part of our emotional circle as caregivers and advisors and, if we choose well, they will both care *for* us and care *about* us. And we, in turn, will care about them.

When Diane was in her fifties, she and her husband moved across the country, back to the small community of

2,500 where they had grown up, to return to their emotional circle. Her husband was ill and they were hoping to get to the bottom of his illness. "We needed to check out his ongoing health issues," Diane says. "We thought we'd get him fixed up and move on, but this was not to be. He was diagnosed with stage 4 lung cancer and less than two years later he passed away. After 40 years of being together, I was now alone." She has no regrets about their decision to move home. "In our time of stress, home was where we needed to be. I am very fortunate to live in a caring community with groups and organizations that hold events and teas and parties, and families support their elderly parents quite a lot. Our town is 75 per cent seniors, and there's not a lot of government support, so it's seniors caring for seniors." Diane appreciates the chance to be near family and has rekindled old ties. "My younger son only lives three hours away and he visits quite often," she says. "He is my 'guardian angel.' As for my older son, although I don't think he will ever come home to live, we do visit each other often. I recently became reconnected with an old friend of my late husband's and mine. He has been by my side these past few months and has been my shoulder to lean on. I don't know if I'll ever remarry, but having a person to be there for you is comforting. As my boys say, 'Mom, you were there when Dad needed you the most, now you have to move on.'"

As Diane watches her mother age, she sees the difference family support can make. "My mother is 80 and about five years ago she moved into a seniors complex where she maintains her independence. My dad passed away at age 61, and if family hadn't been there for her things would have turned out differently. My mom was only 54, but because she had always depended on Dad to do things for her, she was at a real loss. My sister, brother, and I encouraged her to stay in her home and showed her that she was quite capable of looking after herself. Once she gained control of her own life she remained at home for another 20 years. She is still active and says she will never have to move to a nursing home. The support from her family lets her choose how she would like to live. When I'm old, I want the same—a very loving, understanding, and caring family who will take care of my wishes to be as independent as I can for as long as I can."

Mildred had the same goal and, despite serious medical challenges, she was determined to age in place surrounded by her emotional circle. Thanks to the efforts of family and friends, and in particular her son Simon, she was able to realize her dream. After Mildred and her husband retired, they sold their farm and moved to their cottage, which they had converted into a permanent home. By the time Mildred died at age 91, she had lived in this new home for 37 years. During that period she cultivated and drew on a large emotional circle as she nursed her husband through years of Alzheimer's until his death at age 82. Mildred had her own physical problems to contend with, including excruciating pain brought about by a failing hip replacement and the subsequent corrective surgery. Simon remembers her challenges, both immediately post-surgery and long-term. "When she had the surgery," Simon explains, "she was 88 and quite frail and she was left with something called a dropped foot and she had to wear a body brace until she healed. This was very painful, and she could no longer walk on her own, get out of bed, or go to the washroom without assistance. Although she eventually threw the brace away (literally), she always had to use a walker and have someone behind her to steady her balance. And she couldn't stand up or get up from a bed or toilet without assistance."

But Mildred was determined to stay in her house and Simon understood why. "It was her home," he says, "a home that welcomed her family and friends. Neighbours would drop in to visit and when she was no longer able to get up to put on the kettle for tea, they would do it, knowing exactly where everything was in her kitchen. In her home, she was surrounded by her most precious belongings, particularly her flowers. She loved to garden and was president of the horticultural society for many years and her garden was the envy of her neighbours. She enjoyed being surrounded by life—and that is what her home represented to her."

Mildred was able to stay in her home thanks to Simon and other family members and friends, as well as a whole new group of caregivers that Simon organized to support her. "In some ways it was very simple," Simon says. "I knew if she was going to be happy she needed to be in her own home. I also knew that she could never be alone again. That point had been reached and there was no going back."

Simon may call it "simple," but here's his description of what it took to support his mother in her home. "The Ontario government provided two hours a day of caregiving, seven days a week, and they provided case-management support that was invaluable. Through networking, I found someone to stay overnight during the week. We had a little intercom system so my mother could call if she needed to go to the bathroom during the night. The overnight caregiver needed to leave for work in the morning and then the government-provided caregivers would come in and get my mother up and ready for the day. I found several other people who were willing to work during the day. Sometimes Mom would stop cold when she was walking to her room and would collapse on the floor. She wouldn't be injured but she couldn't get up and the support staff wasn't able to lift her. So I found a retired man who lived down the road who was willing to come by on a moment's notice and pick her up. It worked beautifully. He would walk in and say 'Mildred, what are you doing down there?' Then he would proceed to pick her up and get her into bed. On weekends, the family would take turns staying with her or we'd bring her to the cottage with us. For holidays, we would take her to the cottage so the staff could have time off. We had a number of backup people who could come in as needed. I developed a work schedule for all the support staff and set them up as bill payments with the local bank so I could make direct deposits into their bank accounts. To pay for this, I took a line of credit out on Mom's home, and her pension income covered the monthly interest payments. We managed this team for close to four years, until my mother's death."

Simon's approach to grocery shopping illustrates how sensitive he was to maintaining his mother's independence and sense of control over her life. "We would do the grocery shopping for a week or two at a time," Simon explains. "Mom and I would go together and she would use her walker. I would have the cart in one hand and the walker in the other as we made our way around the store. It worked! My mother still felt in charge and could make decisions around what she wanted to have in her cupboards. She always wanted a supply of treats on hand for when friends would drop in to visit and the tea kettle would go on. In her world, people didn't make arrangements to visit, they just dropped by if they were in the neighbourhood. In her mind, nothing changed. She was able to entertain her guests still, in her own home, whenever they came by. That is how she wanted it."

The success of Mildred's strategy was dependent on a number of variables, including the strength and diversity of her emotional circle. "The key factor for me," Simon explains, "was supporting her plan to stay in her own home. Because she always had people calling or dropping in, she was never lonely. That had been her whole life and it didn't change during this time. But the plan depended on me being available to maintain and support the plan 24/7 and being comfortable with all aspects of her care. My brother was not comfortable with the personal care so he was not able to care for Mom over the weekends or during holiday times. We are all different and we just needed to have the right mix to make it work. As for funding this plan, if Mom hadn't had her own home, I am not sure how it would have been financed. Without question, this approach was right for her. She was always a fiercely independent person and although she lost a great deal of her independence after the surgery her mind was still very strong. She needed to maintain her autonomy and have a sense of control over her life, both of which were critically important to her mental and emotional well-being."

When it comes to his own aging, Simon would like to emulate his mother. He is 61 and has been in a committed relationship with his male partner for 14 years. "I would definitely want the same thing for myself," he says. "I couldn't imagine not being in my own space, making decisions that are right for me. But I would not want family doing what I did, unless it was what they truly wanted to do. My mother knew that it was never a burden to me; it was a gift to be able to do this for her. I was so grateful to have this opportunity to give back, and I learned so much about myself during this time. I not only helped her to maintain her quality of life, but improved my own quality of life as well. I would want whoever was taking care of me, either my children, my partner, or my friends, to feel the same way. If I ever felt that I was a burden to people, it would need to end."

Mildred's and Diane's stories speak volumes about the staggering amount of time, effort, finances, and love that can be required to support aging in place, and give us food for thought. Do we have a Simon in our lives who would do the heavy lifting, not to mention the neighbour who would do the actual lifting, or the endless stream of entertaining friends and neighbours? Do we have Diane's close-knit family and supportive community with roots back to her childhood? If not, we may want to consider built-in supports that are part of many housing options we'll be discussing, including homesharing, cohousing, and religious/ethno-cultural and spiritual communities.

Allows for Inter-Generational Connections

We'd be wise to live in a location that is youth-friendly, because connecting with younger people will enrich our lives as we age. Some people with children and grandchildren will make living close to them a priority, while others will focus on being in a place where youngsters want to visit. However, we don't need to be related to young people to benefit from their youthful vim and vigour.

After Debbie made an exploratory visit to a beautiful retirement complex in Arizona, she realized that, for her, proximity to family was going to override her other considerations. "I was impressed with the physical beauty of the surroundings, as well as the architecture of the complex and the thought put into the accommodation," she said. "Every bathroom could accommodate a wheelchair. But I realized that I didn't want to be that far away from my family. If that hadn't been important to me, this could be a fine option. But where I live now, my two daughters and four grandchildren are nearby. Both daughters are homebodies who like family dinners, and access to babysitting, and having grandparents close. So as long as that continues to go well, my choices are local."

For Liz, having a grandchild changed her priorities. "My son, daughter-in-law, and new grandson live six hours away," she says, "and that's too far for regular visits. I don't want to be a stranger to my grandchild. So I'm wondering whether we should move to a community that is closer to them, and we're starting to explore that idea. Even a few hours closer would be better. I don't want to become a full-time grandmother but, if they really needed me, I wouldn't mind spending a week, or whatever, with them. But any place we move would have to be a community I'd want to live in, and one where I'd be happy with or without children nearby. We'll see how it evolves over the next while."

At age 75, Patricia is sharing a triplex with her children and grandchildren, and one of her great joys with the housing arrangement is the way it allows her to stay connected with the younger generations. Four children, from 16 months to 18 years, are growing up in the same house with her. She says her own parents were the inspiration for her multi-generational living. "Dad retired at age 60 after a heart attack," Patricia explains, "and he and my mom moved to an acreage near a small town where they could live more cheaply. The first thing they did was cultivate friends of all ages. They were always having parties and I remember my dad saying, 'When I make my guest list I mix ages and interests and make sure that at least some people don't know each other.' So that's what I learned from them—always make young friends, as well as friends who don't always agree." The huge network her parents had cultivated became even more important when Patricia's dad fell ill again. Patricia remembers her mother telling her, "We're getting pretty exhausted, so friends who volunteer to visit or work in the garden are like a lifeline to us. I don't know what people do who don't have friends to help out." Patricia is confident she'll be able to call on similar support if need be. "When it comes to my future," she says, "I know I will be able to count on my children. I have absolute faith in that. I don't worry about them, or the grandkids, abandoning me. And there are a lot of people in the neighbourhood that I could call on for help. I know at least 60 families in the neighbourhood, people of all ages, many of whom are long-time friends."

At 66 years of age, Pauline is grateful she and her husband chose to retire in a place their grandchildren consider "cool." "Last year our grandsons came to visit us for a week," she explains. "They're preteens and figured life would be pretty boring hanging out with 'the grans,' and they only came because their parents insisted. But we had a surprise up our sleeves. We drove them to a nearby town and signed them up for surfing lessons. They had a fabulous time and they bonded with us forever. Our message is clear: 'If you come and stay with us, we'll take you surfing.' And, no surprise, we're getting to see a lot of them. If you want to see your grandchildren, your retirement location needs serious kid appeal."

Tim and Sandra's location in a small community has a similar allure for their four grandchildren, aged 18 to 12. "The two youngest were just here for two weeks for spring break," Tim says. "The kids really love to come here because at home they have fast-paced lives with all kinds of activities. Here everything operates at a much slower pace. They do skimboarding and explore the tidal pools and play soccer. And the biking is fantastic. They take courses in outdoor education and they even took a course at the Fire Hall. Although we like to travel, we won't go away for March or the summers because we want to spend as much time as possible with the grandchildren."

If we want young visitors, an important consideration is whether our living space can accommodate guests while making both them and us feel at home. A bit of pre-planning could ensure that we can house visitors with minimum disruption to our routine. Solutions vary from a Murphy bed that converts the den into a temporary guest room, to a loft space built over the garage, to a self-standing building on the property. Condos or apartment buildings will often provide suites for guests to rent. And, looking ahead, if we build in a guest space as part of our home, it could provide accommodation for a caregiver down the road.

Opportunities to connect with young people who aren't part of our family can be arranged through organizations such as educational institutions and senior centres. Russ is 77 years of age and has no children but finds that the small city he chose for his retirement offers lots of potential for intergenerational connection. "I'm a mentor with the MBA program at the university and help students get ready to apply for their first job," he explains. "When one of my foreign students got his dream job in the city of his first choice, it was really rewarding. I also mentor high-school students at a nearby school that offers the International Baccalaureate." In Saskatoon, seniors participating with the Sherbrooke Community Centre had the opportunity to work with grade five and six students in A Walk on the Wild Side, a project designed to educate the community about the environment. The seniors helped the students research plants native to the prairie and boreal regions of Saskatchewan. They worked together to design, plant, and maintain community eco-trails and build an insect/butterfly garden for the benefit of Saskatonians and visitors. The project coordinator said that the seniors taught the young people to slow down, listen, reflect, and appreciate the natural environment, and the seniors had the satisfaction of being able to share their expertise.[2]

Municipalities such as Elliot Lake in Northern Ontario argue that the potential for intergenerational connections is what gives them an advantage over age-restricted retirement communities. In its mining days, the town produced most of the world's uranium, and after the mines shut down the community launched a campaign to turn seniors into one of its new industries. The community advertises a comfortable and affordable retirement lifestyle, surrounded by natural beauty, with many of the services and amenities that urban dwellers expect, including arts and culture, clubs, and lifelong learning. All this without the stress of commuting, and little crime and pollution. The emphasis is that Elliot Lake is a "real" place with lots of younger residents and many children. But since older people make up a significant percentage of the population, there are many services that cater to them, but with a different feel than in a community purpose-built for seniors. The town has attracted two thousand retirees from all over Canada, the United States, and Europe.[3]

Gives a Sense of Community

In addition to housing us, our home is also a bridge that connects us to our community. One of the great risk factors of living in one's own home is social isolation. The research into the heat-wave deaths in France in 2003 revealed that, along with health and housing conditions, social factors contributed to the deaths of the seniors. The risk of death was multiplied by a factor of six for those people who did not participate in social, religious, cultural, or leisure activities. The disaster raised the issue of the isolation of the elderly in French society in general, an isolation that was further exacerbated by the timing of the crisis. Because the heat wave happened in August, many people were away on holiday, including health officials and family members.[4]

A geriatric psychiatrist told me that isolation is one of the biggest issues facing her senior patients who are still living in their homes. And one of their biggest regrets is ignoring opportunities they had earlier in their lives to create more connections with others. Loneliness has a greater impact on us than mere bad feelings: it can hasten our death. Research conducted by Cornell University concluded that loneliness produces changes in the body that mimic the aging process and increase the risk of heart disease. While earlier studies had found a link between loneliness and stress-induced changes in cardiovascular responses, this was the first to establish that persistence of loneliness over time sets the stage for health problems in later life. Anthony Ong, associate professor of human development in Cornell University's College of Human Ecology and the study's co-author, says, "I think one of the most important and life-affirming messages of this research is the reminder that we all desire and need meaningful social connections."[5]

Given the importance of feeling part of a community as we age, we'll need to keep a sharp eye on whether our surroundings provide us with this sense of belonging. If we're moving to a new location we'll want to scope out the community gathering places—coffee shops, libraries, and community centres. How sociable are people? Do strangers smile and say hello? Do people sitting next to each other on a park bench feel free to strike up a conversation? How are community decisions made? Is there a residents' association? If you're moving to a condo or an apartment building, are there common spaces designed to encourage mingling? In *Unassisted Living: Ageless Homes for Later Life*, Wid Chapman and Jeffrey Rosenfeld describe how neighbours living in row houses in San Diego became friends when postal service was denied to their front doors. The architect placed free-standing apartment-style mailboxes in the courtyard of the complex and added some benches, and this became the spot to congregate and socialize.[6] A friend of mine decided to improve her own neighbourliness by reinstating the front porch that had been removed from her house in an earlier renovation. By sitting on her porch she signals that she is at home and welcoming guests, and having good sightlines to the street gives her great opportunities to chat with pass-ersby.

Liz moved to a small village when she was 62 and retired and says the true friendliness of a small town is hard to judge until you live there. "My whole concept of friendship was around my workplace and I didn't realize how much I would miss having working colleagues," she says. "It's very different making friends after you've retired and no longer have the workplace context. You have no professional status and it's a little bit like being back in the schoolyard—rather competitive and silly. Also, when local issues arise, if you line yourself up on the wrong side you can be ostracized. And the people who don't want change are not the locals; it's the relative newcomers. What has saved me is my con-nection to a bigger, wider community beyond this small town. And I've also been enjoying the people I've met vol-unteering for the food bank."

In contrast, Tim and Sandra were overwhelmed (in a good way) by the friendliness of the small town they retired to when they were in their mid-fifties. "When we got here, we didn't know anybody," Sandra explains. "But people are really friendly. There are 59 or 60 clubs or boards you could join in this community, but it was the seniors group New Horizons that really saved me. The first meeting I attended, there were a hundred people. I go to yoga and Pilates there, I do the bird count, and I'm working on a club newsletter.

Tim's hobby is winemaking and he joined the wine club."

When assessing a community it's instructive to revisit the writing of the visionary and activist Jane Jacobs, who got people thinking about the way they relate to one another with her groundbreaking book *The Death and Life of Great American Cities*. Jacobs talked about the importance of eyes upon the neighbourhood—buildings oriented so that they face outward rather than with their backs to the street, and busy sidewalks. As she wrote, "Nobody enjoys sitting on a stoop or looking out a window at an empty street. Almost nobody does such a thing. Large numbers of people entertain themselves, off and on, by watching street activity."[7]

Keeps Us Growing and Learning

Where we live should provide opportunities for growth and learning, whether formal or informal. Recognizing the importance of continuing education to aging boomers, some retirement communities are being located on or near campuses of educational institutions. The *New York Times* reported that in 2007 in the United States there were more than 50 retirement communities located on or near college campuses.[8] In addition to easy access to courses and continuing education, seniors can benefit from the recreational and cultural services that serve the student body. Communities with academic institutions may also offer good health care because of medical schools and teaching hospitals.

At 87 years of age, Sandy decided to leave the basement apartment where he had been living in his daughter's home and move into a retirement residence with ties to a nearby university. The residence contains a classroom that is linked to the university network and offers seminars and lectures. Whenever the weather permits, Sandy goes out on his scooter and heads for the university. He has toured every corner of the campus. "I like the academic aspects of this residence," Sandy says. "I taught high school for 30 years and I'm going to offer some courses to the other residents. I'd like to offer woodworking and art classes. I have my own woodworking tools and some clay for sculpture. I love creating things, and with my courses I want to make things happen for other people, otherwise the days are long. I was lonely living with my daughter, especially when they had parties upstairs, and I came here for the people. For the first three weeks after I moved, I really regretted the decision because everybody is old. But now I'm sitting with different groups and we're really starting to come together."

Patricia learned the importance of personal growth by watching her parents age. "Their approach," she explains, "was to learn something new every day. They were completely open to new things, new ideas, and new adventures." Patricia kept this in mind when she decided to sign up for riding lessons at age 65. A decade later she rides every other week and she's aiming to get to weekly. "My love affair with horses started when I was nine years old and my parents paid for 10 lessons," she remembers. "After that I was allowed to gallop to and from school, but I didn't really know what I was doing. Despite falling in love with horses at such an early age, I only had sporadic contact with horses until my granddaughter turned eight. I decided to sign her up for riding camp and I would drive her over and stay and watch—and drool. It was such an inspiration that when I signed her up for lessons in the fall, I signed myself up too. My ability to lose myself in my horseback riding has become a great strength in moments of stress. It really regenerates me."

When it comes to opportunities for learning and growth, many of us can't imagine a future without access to cultural or artistic activities. Marcie is 71, and her sons have asked her to leave her apartment in the city and move closer to them. But for Marcie the deal breaker is that their small community has no live theatre. "You have to drive to the nearby town just to see a movie," she says. "The town is talking about a big downtown revitalization that is supposed to include a theatre. But I'm going to wait and see."

Artistic and cultural activities were the magnets that drew Adele to move to her small town. "A community with artists has hearts and interesting brains," she says, "which leads to good conversations and projects worth doing."

For Patricia, it's the big city that lets her stretch artistically. In addition to her horseback riding, she takes advantage of art courses offered by the university's continuing education program and has access to a nearby community centre. "I'm part of a painting group that started decades ago," she says. "About 10 of us rent space together about three times per month in the community centre and we're there from 9:30 a.m. to 2 p.m. We're all painters and one of us has turned into a photographer. The youngest is 68 and the oldest is well into her eighties. Once a month, we bring in our paintings for comment. We have learned to criticize each other constructively, and how to push each other to go beyond where we'd normally go."

Finding intellectual stimulation can become harder in our later years. Julia has been watching the challenges her mother faces at 85 because she is still so mentally able. Her retirement home is meeting her mother's social needs, but not her intellectual ones. But Julia is well aware of the challenges. "As my mother will admit," Julia says, "she now tends to fall asleep at lectures, movies, or even at her beloved concerts. Her main occupations (beside family and friends, mostly via telephone) are reading, listening to music on the radio, and watching from her window. What she really needs are people with whom to have reasonably interesting conversations on a one-to-one basis." Julia has an idea that she thinks might address this issue. "I'm imagining something like an inventory or listing of seniors in the city who would be interested in meeting others to discuss particular subject areas—history, literature, the immigrant experience, whatever," she explains. "Of course, so much depends on personal chemistry as to whether two people would get along, but if they did manage to link up, conversations could be carried on by phone as well, which would make it easier to sustain the conversation and the relationship."

In some communities, a seniors centre provides opportunities to grow and learn, and might be able to provide some of the intellectual connections that Julia would like to see for her mother. Brock House Society (www.brock housesociety.com) is a non-profit organization in Vancouver founded in 1974 to preserve and restore the heritage building of Brock House and to operate as a seniors activity centre. The list of activities runs for pages, with a random sample including film night, mah-jong, Pilates, opera, play reading, conversational French, and woodworking. Volunteers serve in a range of capacities, as greeters, office staff, cafeteria servers, librarians, woodworkers, summer and winter fair organizers and helpers, musicians, entertainers, social organizers, as well as on the many committees, and as directors and executives. The building is owned by the City of Vancouver and the society shares the building with a restaurant. During the weekdays the members use the building to socialize and enjoy a program of activities. In the evenings and on weekends, the restaurant uses the building and shares the costs of maintenance and furnishings.

Provides Easy Access to Services and Amenities

We need our home to allow easy access to basic services such as a doctor, a dentist, a grocery store, a bank, a pharmacy, a post office, and a library. Our personal list of "must haves" might include a farmer's market, a liquor store, a bookstore, a place of worship, a yoga studio, a pub, barber/beauty shop, a massage therapist, dry cleaners, a coffee shop, a theatre, an art gallery, a performance hall, a sports arena, and restaurants. At age 75, Patricia says that being a 10-minute walk from Tai Chi is very important. "I took up Tai Chi with my father," she explains. "After my mother died in 1993, I spent a lot of time with him, and went to his classes with him. He lived four years after her death. Not too long after his death I found classes at the YWCA, which were the same kind as his. I go to them every Saturday, and Monday morning, and, if I can, Tuesday evening."

To reach our services while we can still drive, we'll need road systems that are forgiving of failing eyesight and slower reaction times. This rules out major highways and driveways with difficult access to busy streets. And we'll need public transportation that is accessible and affordable. When we're on foot, we'll want to be able to travel through neighbourhoods where we won't fear for our personal safety, and walk on sidewalks and pathways that are level and well lit. And we'll need traffic lights that make allowance for slower pedestrians. One of my aunt Jean's great frustrations as she aged was the very fast timing of the traffic light that stood between her and her favourite restaurant. Because the crosswalk light would turn red when she was only halfway through the intersection, she was too frightened to cross the busy street alone. When I was with her, we would link arms and brace ourselves for the extreme sport, with me reassuring her that the cars wouldn't deliberately hit us—would they?

Glenda and Dwight are delighted with the variety of services they can access in their community, and the fact that many of them are geared to seniors. They are both 75 years old and for the past seven years they have been living in a small town where about 40 per cent of the population is over the age of 65. "I'll give you an idea of what's available," Glenda says. "Our grocery store delivers, as well as another wonderful prepared food service with a large variety of meals that you just pop in the microwave. We have a foot care nurse who comes to see us, and a nursing service drives around in a pink car, visiting patients. When our 83-year-old friend fell and broke her hip, the clinic provided her with daycare and her church group made up a schedule for volunteers to help her out. My yoga class is run by a 70-year-old woman. For the past five years, a group of us have been meeting weekly to make crafts to sell to support an international charity, and the friendships have grown very strong. And the town is big enough to be included on tours like the youth symphony so we got to billet two young men, one who plays the cello and the other the tuba, and it was great fun transporting them in our small car." Although not everything is within easy walking distance of their home, this is not worrying them. "We're five minutes by car to anything important—lab, doctor, dentist," Glenda explains. "The town is launching a volunteer taxi service. Dwight has volunteered to be a driver while he still can and he's passed the criminal check. At some point, hopefully way down the road, we'll likely become customers for the service." Here's how their 50-year-old daughter assesses her parents' relocation. "This place really agrees with them," she says. "Since they moved here, they seem to be getting younger every year. I've never seen them so happy."

In contrast, Lorna, at age 65, has been spending weekends and holidays in her and her husband's renovated farmhouse. Although they modified it for senior living, she has come to the conclusion it would be far better to retire in their city home. "If I lived here in the country, I'd be in the car all the time," she explains. "I like to swim every day, and there's no place to swim. The closest gym is miles away. There's no entertainment, and even the library is being relocated farther down the road. This is very different from my city home, where everything is so convenient. To access the services we want and need, we'll have to change our retirement plans and focus on our city home." To make this work, Lorna has come up with a creative option that is discussed in Supportive Housing.

Is Beautiful to the Eye, Good for the Soul, and Energizing for the Body

Beautiful surroundings are important to most of us, but some people seem to be more sensitive to ugliness than others. And, of course, beauty is in the eye of the beholder. So while some people may think that the constant stream of traffic on the freeway is poetry in motion, others find beauty in the natural world. It is important to acknowledge the degree to which beauty matters to us and factor that into our housing decisions. Liz knows that, although her partner could live anywhere, she is very house-proud. "I am an aesthete and highly sensitivity to beauty, so certain choices that may be very practical for us for aging well— like a bungalow right on the road—are just ruled out. I need beauty and I love this village because of the river and all the deciduous trees around me. My partner respects cleanliness and order and is much more practical. He likes to mow grass and he doesn't obsess about the design of things. So this property is perfect for both of us—a stone house with a beautiful garden and a lawn to mow and shrubs to clip. We did our homework before we chose this community. There are good medical facilities, all the beautiful walking trails by the river are flat, and everything is very convenient. This is by far the cheapest, most practical, and most beautiful place we could have moved to."

For many of us, being near nature is a very high priority. We may want to be near water or within walking distance of a park or be able to see trees out our window. It feels good to get into the beauty of nature and it also keeps us healthy. ENABLE-AGE, a longitudinal study funded by the European Union to look at the relationship between our home environment and healthy aging, surveyed nearly two thousand people in five member countries. They were between 75 and 89 years of age and living alone in their own homes in urban areas. Participants said that an important factor in remaining healthy was to be able to get outdoors on a regular basis. In all countries, barriers to getting outdoors, including accessibility problems in the entrances of people's homes, correlated to poorer perceived health.[9]

When Russ retired at age 65, he chose a place that he admits "doesn't have much sizzle," but he loves its access to nature. "This is not a place with a lot of sophistication," he says. "But in the big city where I used to live, I really missed the outdoors and the greenery. I've made a habit of leaving town every Sunday to go biking or hiking. It's so nice to get away. I have a lady friend who's very keen on hiking and she's picking up cross-country skiing. We met in a garden group. I'm 77 and she's seven years younger and very fit and walks long distances. So proximity to nature is very important to both of us."

When Alice moved from a rural property into the heart of a small city in her fifties, staying connected to the natural world was her priority. "I'm 79 years old and use crutches for support. I've got to have my freedom, my independence, and that's why I use my crutches," she explains. "Otherwise I wouldn't walk. Where we live is very convenient. Everything is within walking distance and I don't need a car. I garden and raise most of my vegetables and trade garlic with the neighbours, and every Sunday we walk in the woods by the lake. It's very important that I stay in touch with nature, and that's possible even in the middle of a city."

Gary was looking for access to nature and, ironically, found it easier to find in a city than in a small town surrounded by wilderness. "When I first retired I moved to a small community where I imagined having great access to the outdoors," he explains. "There were mountains and forest all around us, so I just assumed it would be easy to get into the wild. But once we moved there, I realized I had to drive half an hour to get to a good hike. I'm a great walker and this was a great disappointment. I had been expecting that access to the natural beauty would be my compensation for the isolation of the community. But I could only stare at it from a distance." Now 72, Gary has relocated to a small city and has been delighted to find how much easier it is to get outdoors. "Here I don't even need a car," he explains. "There are superb walks everywhere."

If we want to encourage our community to create parks that are better for aging minds and bodies, we could follow the lead of the Seniors Health Promotion Coalition in Ottawa. During Active Aging Week in September, they encourage people to assess their local park on its suitability for older adults to be active, and to suggest improvements. People are asked to complete an Age Friendly Checklist and send their results and photos back to the coalition, with prizes offered for participation. The feedback and ideas are used by the coalition to help build and support future park use by older adults. In 2011, six parks were assessed by 81 older adults, mainly in the 65 to 79 age group. Their suggestions included installing benches with supporting arms along pathways in a way that supports conversations, public washrooms, signage, a gazebo or other outside covered area, and intergenerational activities.[10]

Accommodates Our Animals

Many of us have animals that are part of our lives, and if they aren't happy we aren't happy. Marcie was 70 years old when she got her first dog. "I'd been alone for 20 years and I finally got a pet," she says. "I live in the moment and I realized that I needed some responsibility to provide my life with an anchor. So now I have a dog that I have to walk, and he'll be part of any future housing decisions." Dog amenities have become important as well for Patricia, who at 75 also got her dog late in life. "Having a dog was a big change and it forces me to get exercise," she says. "I live in the middle of the city and it's very important to me now that I live 10 minutes from a huge park that is dog-friendly. One downside is that I have to think about having someone take care of the dog when I'm away." Glenda and Dwight also factored in their animals when they relocated. "We were in our late sixties when we relocated to this small town. It has excellent amenities for dogs and we picked a bungalow that is located about five minutes' walk from a nature reserve, and the nearby civic centre has an off-leash dog walk."

Elizabeth didn't expect to wind up "in an old folks home," and certainly not at age 74, but a big factor in her happiness has been being able to keep her animals with her. A nearly fatal illness followed by a lengthy stay in rehab meant that she was no longer able to live on her own. Her daughters helped her sell her condo and with the proceeds she was able to afford a retirement home for people who can function in an independent living setting. She sees both the pros and cons of this turn of events. She had been living on her own after a divorce 30 years earlier and found it to be an education "to live amongst a group of people whom I did not choose to be my daily friends and companions." Although she misses the amenities of her condo she still has her car and her dog and is almost as independent as she used to be. "I count myself as fortunate indeed," she says, "that I have landed in a good house where I have found a few new friends and can get help, should I need it, in a matter of minutes."[11]

When Alice was 53, she and her dog moved across the country to a small city on the west coast. "I had been living a rural life, six miles from a small town, and I was almost living off the grid," she explains. "I had raised my children in a big city but, after my divorce, I moved to the country and I found that I loved living in near-wilderness. I loved the forest, the pond, and canoeing up the creek. I found that nature was part of my being. But here I was, over 50 and alone, and I wasn't strong enough to live like that any more on my own." When she landed in the city she didn't know a soul and her dog was her only companion. "I lived in my truck with my dog until I could find an apartment that accepted dogs," she remembers. "I've always been an activist and it didn't take me long to find my community, but I have no intention of ever being without canine companionship." Alice is now 79 and has two dogs, a standard poodle and a small mixed breed. "I overlap them with one being much older than the other," she explains. "That way, I won't ever be without a dog. If I go into a home, it will have to be one that accepts one dog and maybe two."

A seniors cohousing complex in Saskatoon called Wolf Willow would meet Alice's criteria. The project acknowledges the importance of our animals by permitting each resident to have two pets. You'll read about the newly launched Wolf Willow in the upcoming section on cohousing.

Makes Us Feel at Home

When I think about feeling at home the word that comes to mind is *gezellig*. My in-laws are from the Netherlands and, although they speak English fluently, this is one of the few words they throw into a conversation without translation when they want to refer to something as *cozy*. English doesn't have one word that captures *gezellig*'s full connotation of *convivial* and *being at home*. *Gezellig* means "home is where the heart is." When you are at home, you have a sense of belonging and feel you can be truly and completely yourself. While there are some excellent tools out there to help you assess cities in terms of characteristics such as affordability and amenities, the real intangible is figuring out where you feel *gezellig*. When you walk down the streets or sit in the coffee shops or chat with the neighbours do you have a sense of belonging? Will the community welcome, or at least tolerate, your personal choices, whether they be lifestyle or fashion style? Can you be your most authentic self? At 75 years of age, Glenda lives in a small town where about 40 per cent of the population is over the age of 65. One of the things that makes her feel at home is the fact that things are so casual. "You don't have to worry about what you're going to wear," she says.

When it comes to sitting down and conversing with your neighbours are there enough people who share your world view that you can find common ground? Can you speak your deepest beliefs and feel that you will be understood? Let's look at two examples from either end of the political spectrum where people found the answer to this question was "no." A dynamic retired marketing manager decided to pull up stakes and leave the big city for an idyllic island life. The community she had chosen was known for a lifestyle focused on healthy living and environmental consciousness. It proved to be a bad fit, being too counterculture for her sensibilities. She rushed back to her city life saying, "If I ever have another discussion about bowel cleansing, I will have to do myself in." Then there's the policy consultant who began to spend weeks in a sunny, wealthy retirement community because his wife hated winter. He found the right-wing perspectives of the residents hard to take and couldn't find people who shared his values. He and his wife agreed to spend a bit more time apart. She would still go south but spend less time in those warmer climes, and he would make alternative plans for those weeks.

When Gary turned 65, he and his wife moved to the west coast to be closer to their daughter and enjoy the milder weather. They visited a number of small communities before picking one, and then built a house. Looking back, Gary feels their decision was too hasty. "We committed ourselves far too soon and far too extensively," he says. "We had our hearts set on a waterfront property and found it surprisingly difficult. Finally we got a plot of land that we could afford, but we never consciously chose that community. I had no idea how isolated it was. I hadn't thought through how I wanted to live and how I wanted to spend my time. The move turned out to be a terrible mistake. I expected to have intellectual discussions with people but found very few with whom I could carry on a conversation. For the most part, people had little education and no ambition. And they didn't like people like us moving in, so they weren't particularly welcoming. It wasn't a positive, upbeat atmosphere. When I look back, I realize it was a case of the tail wagging the dog. We focused on the waterfront location and the availability of a place we could afford and I just figured the rest would work out. In hindsight, I wish we'd thought the thing through and focused on the full implications of our decision." Now 72, Gary has relocated to a small city and finally feels at home. "I feel I've found my community," he explains. "This area is full of well-educated people and they're the kind of ambitious people with positive attitudes that I'm used to. The area I've moved into is very orientated toward its older people and very supportive of them. I've joined a group that meets regularly for dinner and a movie and I see myself finding some kindred spirits or, at least, people to talk to." His wife decided to stay put in the small community and they have gone their separate ways.

You may have found a compatible city or town, but what about your immediate surroundings? If you're living in a retirement community, are you comfortable with bylaws that may restrict buyers to certain ages, or prohibit children or pets? If you're looking at living in an apartment or buying a condo, does it have a welcoming atmosphere? The following story from the *Toronto Star* gives you a sense of how the attitude of some condo owners could cast a cold chill over a sense of community. A condo resident wrote to ask an expert in condo law whether the property manager had the right to prevent some women residents from sitting in the lobby and having a chat. According to the writer, the manager had received complaints that the women's presence was compromising the privacy of those meeting with the manager, even though her office had a door. The lawyer explained that condo owners are allowed to make reasonable use of the common areas and "sitting on lobby chairs or couches would appear to be a reasonable use." He advised that if the condo board were to pass a rule prohibiting such use, it would probably not be approved by the courts.[12] The fact that some condo owners don't want to see people enjoying the lobby speaks eloquently about the atmosphere they hope to establish.

Hold out for your version of *gezellig*. In researching this book I've found a remarkable number of unique housing options. If they haven't come to your community yet, there may soon be a sufficient mass of like-minded people to make it happen. The following examples will give you a sense of the range of possibilities. Yarrow, British Columbia, used to be its own town before being incorporated into Chilliwack and eventually losing its town centre. Under the leadership of the Yarrow Ecovillage Society (YES) Cooperative, a site on Yarrow Central Road is being developed to include a 28-unit cohousing project, a village centre, seniors cohousing, a learning centre, and an organic farm. The organizers have put out a call for seniors who want to design their own community through a process that would involve a series of six workshops over eight months. At the conclusion of the process, participants would have the opportunity to purchase a unit.[13]

BOOM (www.boomforlife.com) is a $250-million development in Rancho Mirage near Palm Springs being built to house 800 people. Originally conceived as a retirement community for the lesbian, gay, bisexual, and transgender population, the project has evolved to be open for all, with a focus on those over 40. Plans include a boutique hotel, a health spa and wellness centre, as well as a playground for visiting grandchildren. In an interview, Matthias Hollwich, the lead architect, explained the impetus for the project. "BOOM started with the LGBT community in mind, because they are mavericks, have a different definition of family, and there is even more age discrimination than in the straight community."[14] Other BOOM residential communities are planned for Spain and New York City.

If I develop dementia I'd like to move to a place like the Hogewey complex in Weesp, The Netherlands, population 18,000. The 23-unit apartment complex includes a small supermarket, restaurant, café, and theatre—all amenities that are used by the neighbouring community. The staff members wear street clothes, mobile kitchens close to the living quarters generate the smells of home cooking, and there are lots of communal spaces including a flower-filled courtyard. The residents, despite their mental challenges, are encouraged to grocery shop, assist with the laundry, and help one another as part of their daily routine. The philosophy behind Hogewey is that patients suffer less stress if they are in more homelike surroundings and kept as active as their condition allows.[15]

Lets Us Live Green

We'd be smart to look for environmentally sensitive communities and housing designs. They have the potential to lower our home's operating costs at the same time as they reduce our impact on the planet. If we are adapting our own home for the long term, we can take advantage of energy-saving strategies, and if we are seeking out a seniors community, we can look for one that is eco-friendly. Incorporating green and sustainable features into our building plans might mean retrofitting for energy and water conservation through the use of geothermal techniques and rainwater catchment, and the use of alternate energy sources such as wind or solar. The need for air conditioning can be reduced through design principles—roof overhangs, the efficient use of cross-ventilation, and techniques such as geothermal coils for heat displacement.

Wolf Creek Lodge, a seniors cohousing community in Grass Valley, California, is an example of an innovative approach to environmental and social sustainability. (Cohousing is a form of accommodation that creates a neighbourhood where seniors can support each other, as discussed in the upcoming section Cohousing.) The community is located on 3.5 acres of open space along Wolf Creek, within walking distance of stores and restaurants. The buildings were designed to be extremely energy-efficient, with solar panels providing hot water for the hydronic heating system, passive cooling that eliminates the need for air conditioners using fans, cross ventilation, and radiant barriers, and low electricity use through energy-efficient lighting and good day-lighting. As a result, monthly energy bills are estimated to be minimal (about $20). Construction has given priority to building materials that minimize the impact on the environment and indoor air quality.[16]

In British Columbia, the non-profit organization SAFER-Home, (www.saferhomesociety.com) promotes sustainable, healthy, and safe building standards by certifying houses that meet its standards. The acronym stands for Sustainable, Automated, Friendly, Environmental, Recycling. The 19-point SAFERHome standards address issues such as placement and positioning of electrical outlets, positioning of light switches, bath and shower controls, door and hallway widths, and other considerations that would assist aging in place. Some of the electrical wiring standards could allow for energy savings. While the entire program could be costly to integrate into an existing home, you could look for the SAFER certification when purchasing a new home or build a new home to SAFER standards with the goal of achieving certification.

Modifying Our Home

WHETHER we stay put or relocate, we'll need a home that supports us as we age. Accommodation that can adapt to an aging body and mind will help us maintain our independence. If we lose our muscle strength, we'll appreciate latches that can work with arthritic hands. If our eyesight is failing, we'll be glad of bright lights to help us see more clearly. If our home is free of hazards, such as scatter rugs or risers on the thresholds, we'll lessen our chances of tripping and injuring ourselves. And if a medical emergency requires us to use a walker or wheelchair, we'll be able to recuperate at home if we can get through the front door, manoeuvre ourselves in and out of bed, and take showers.

ENABLE-AGE, the longitudinal study referred to earlier that looked at the relationship between our home environment and healthy aging, found that seniors who were living in more accessible and usable homes, and who perceived their home as meaningful, had a better sense of well-being. The concept of *meaningful* in this context is an acknowledgement that the appropriateness of someone's home has a subjective component, so that something viewed as an accessibility barrier might be a precious object that is important for the person's well-being.[1] The researchers concluded that making modifications to one's home to help compensate for declines in older age is very important in order to maintain independence and a healthy state. They found that for many people being able to stay in familiar surroundings helped them avoid problems that were common in later life, such as falls and depression.[2]

I have watched design barriers at work in my own home when we've entertained friends who were using canes, crutches, or wheelchairs. To reach our house from the street you must first surmount the high curb, climb several uneven stone steps, and manoeuvre along a charming but rough stone path. Before gaining the front door, you must step up onto a porch and then over the doorstep. Having finally entered the house you can't let your guard down, for between the foyer and the hall there is a small riser that seems designed for tripping. There is no ground floor bathroom; if you need to use the washroom you must climb either up a floor or down a floor, in both cases using steep stairways without handrails. There is no bedroom on the ground floor so reaching sleeping accommodation requires the same risk-taking. Instead of a shower stall, the guest bathroom has a bathtub, and there are no grab bars on either bath or toilet. I took a few minutes to scan the house for features I find challenging even at my relatively able-bodied stage. They are numerous: to reach the upper shelves of the kitchen cupboards I have to climb onto the counter; opening the garage door takes every ounce of my strength; the environmentally-approved light bulbs in several rooms are too dim to allow me to see properly; I can't turn the stiff outside hose faucet on and off without using a jury-rigged tool . . . and I could go on. Probably most significantly, our house is spread over four storeys, counting the basement where our washer and dryer are located.

Phil is 80 years old. He says that if I do nothing else, I should redesign things so that I could live on one level if something happens. To be accurate, he says, "*when* something happens." When he was diagnosed with pulmonary fibrosis last year, he was grateful to be living in a one-floor ranch-style house. "Whatever else you do with your home, get onto one level," he urges. "Things can happen to you that you would never anticipate—like a broken ankle, like pulmonary fibrosis. Old age doesn't come alone. It comes with other things that hit you from many different angles."

But most of us cringe at the thought of living in accommodation that looks like a hospital or feels like an institution—even if it might mean living longer in our home. Happily, thanks to *universal design*, we can plan for a future of less personal capacity *and* live elegantly. We don't have to choose. Designers and architects use *universal design* or *design for all* principles to create living spaces that are adaptable, easy, and open, as well as barrier-free. The objective of universal design is to create products and environments that can be used by people of all ages with diverse abilities, without segregating or stigmatizing any users.[3] A good example is the dropped curb, which is appreciated equally by people in wheelchairs or scooters, parents pushing baby carriages, or travellers struggling with heavy luggage. The goal is to achieve universal design objectives in our home, while creating a place of beauty. Let's take the washroom as an example of the universal design approach. Toilet seats are at the comfort height of 18 inches rather than the standard 14-inch, sinks are higher to allow leg room below, showers have seats and are curbless with the floor sloping slightly to the drain, and the shower head is adjustable. Handles are levered instead of round, storage spaces are conveniently located, lighting is plentiful, and electrical outlets are 18 to 24 inches from the floor for easier access. The doors are 36 inches wide rather than the standard 32 or 34 inches to accommodate wheelchairs, and they either slide into pockets, or lie flat against the wall and open out. As for those grab bars, if you add structural support behind the wall, you don't need to install them right away—they can be added if needed. The resulting look could be plucked from a contemporary design magazine.

There are a number of resources to help us assess our home and make these modifications. *The Safe Living Guide: A Guide to Home Safety for Seniors*, published by the Public Health Agency of Canada, includes checklists that identify hazards both outside and inside the home, as well as tips for safety improvements and case studies to illustrate how safety changes or adaptations can help older adults live more safely and healthily.[4] *Maintaining Seniors' Independence Through Home Adaptations: A Self-Assessment Guide*, published by Canada Mortgage and Housing Corporation (CMHC), uses checklists to walk us through our living space by room and by activity with drawings to illustrate the suggested modifications. For example, if we are having difficulty using the stairs, there is a range of suggested solutions from relocating the bedroom, bathroom, or laundry room, to improving lighting and replacing stair coverings.[5] In addition, CMHC publishes a more extensive home adaptation tool, *Maintaining Seniors' Independence—A Guide to Home Adaptations*, which is designed for use by an occupational therapist but could be used by anyone.[6] The guide includes an assessment tool and three case studies that illustrate simple, inexpensive modifications. There are a number of information sheets about specific modifications, including ramps, elevators, and home automation, as well as design guidelines for accessible homes.[7]

The Hartford Financial Services Group has published a number of useful publications, many of which were developed from research conducted with the MIT AgeLab. *Modern Ideas, Modern Living: Taking the Next Step in Home Design and Planning for the Lifestyle You Want* encourages you to think about the next step in your lifestyle and how to ensure that your home will fit you. The ideas are designed to help you work through the options and talk with people who are important to you about these decisions. They also publish *Simple Solutions: Practical Ideas and Products to Enhance Independent Living*, a guidebook featuring some 200 simple design ideas and household products to make your home more comfortable, convenient, and safe.[8] If you'd like some professional assistance in evaluating your home for pitfalls, some government programs provide an occupational therapist to conduct a home assessment, and, depending on circumstances, some of the cost might be subsidized.

If you're still not convinced that your home can be both lovely to look at as well as designed for the long run, have a look at *Unassisted Living: Ageless Homes for Later Life* by Wid Chapman and Jeffrey Rosenfeld. Chapman is an architect and Rosenfeld is a professor of gerontology and their book includes architectural renderings and photos of 33 gorgeous homes that promote active aging. Their examples run the gamut of aging boomers' interests, including urban and rural settings, focus on sustainability, complex families and non-traditional households, and communities based on spirituality or shared interests. The homes they feature "are places where people will be living on their own, usually with people they love and enjoy, with the expectation of longer, healthier lives."[9] In addition, they are beautifully designed.

While we're doing these modifications, let's dream big. Even working within a limited budget we might be able to explore new interests or invest existing interests with new vigour. We might soundproof a room for band practice, carve out a yoga and meditation space, or renovate a loft for artistic pursuits.

If you decide to renovate, you may be eligible for government funding. Depending on where you live and your income level, there are a variety of programs that provide financial support for modifications that assist people to age in their own homes. For example, the Nova Scotia's Home Adaptations for Seniors' Independence (HASI) program helps low-income seniors pay for home modifications to extend the time they can live in their own homes. Eligible adaptations include handrails in hallways and stairways, easy-to-reach work and storage areas in the kitchen, lever handles on doors, walk-in showers with grab bars, and bathtub grab bars and seats.[10] The Saskatchewan Housing Corporation has a number of programs to support seniors living at home, including modifications for disabilities, some repairs, and some energy upgrades.[11] If your home requires extensive modifications, such as widening doorways and increasing space for wheelchair manoeuvring, you may qualify for federal assistance under the Residential Rehabilitation Assistance Program for Persons with Disabilities.[12]

If you need to modify your home, it's important to tackle the job while you can still adjust to the changes. Lorna and her husband inherited his mother's rural property and are currently using it as a vacation property. Thinking it would be their retirement home, they did a major renovation, including a master suite built to accommodate seniors. They were hoping that Lorna's mother-in-law would be comfortable staying by herself in the property, but it proved too late for her to adjust to the radical changes. "She is 88 years old and had lived on the farm for 65 years," Lorna explains. "We gutted the home and everything is brand spanking new. Because we couldn't have gas, we installed an induction countertop stove. She would have needed to have gotten used to these changes years ago—it didn't happen soon enough—so we can't leave her alone there now. She's moved out to an apartment several kilometres away where she's much safer."

Several of the options discussed below involve home-sharing, and if you decide to go that route you would want to build the appropriate space into your renovation plans. If you are considering sharing your home you need to check for zoning restrictions since some jurisdictions restrict the number of unrelated people living in the same house.[13] As well, your requirements may vary over time. For example, you may start out renting space in your home to a tenant and, down the road, convert it into a space for a caregiver. Having space to accommodate a caregiver, especially if it were attractive space, might put you at an advantage in a competitive market. Here we can look to Victoria, British Columbia, for a vision of the future. With nearly 18 per cent of its population seniors, Victoria is our "oldest" metropolitan area, and caregivers are at a premium. An 86-year-old long-time resident of the city told me that she and her friends are finding it harder and harder to find household help, and this is threatening people's ability to stay in their homes. To emphasize how bad the situation has become, she recounts the following story, which she swears is true. "The husband of a friend of mine was having an affair with the cleaning lady. When my friend found out, she had the toughest decision to make. Should she get rid of the husband or the cleaning lady? She decided to keep the husband but, I can tell you, it wasn't an easy choice."

Home modifications are not merely nice to have. In a medical crisis, they can mean the difference between home care and institutional care. After my mother broke her collarbone, home care may well have been an option if my parents had agreed to modify their home. At the very least, they could have reduced the number of moves they ended up making and spent fewer years in long-term care facilities.

Community Support

HAVING a living space adapted to our needs will help us stay independent for the long term, but it won't be enough. If we want to age in place, we won't be able to do it alone. We'll need companionship as well as help with a multitude of everyday challenges: chores, meal preparation, shopping, home repairs, and getting to appointments. The ENABLE-AGE study referred to earlier, which looked at the relationship between your home environment and healthy aging, confirms the kind of support needed to age in place and maintain your quality of life. Researchers asked seniors whether they had access to help and support in three key areas: assistive devices (e.g., mobility devices and technologies for hearing and visual impairments), care services (health and social care), and informal care (family, friends et cetera). Two-thirds of the seniors reported that all their needs were met. The one-third with unfulfilled needs most commonly focused on a lack of assistive devices. Only a small proportion of people reported that they did not have a support person available to help them.[1]

Although provincial and territorial governments provide a variety of home care programs to help seniors meet some of these needs, people often need to supplement them with their own resources.[2] In many communities, organizations have sprung up to fill some of the gap. For over 25 years, the non-profit organization SPRINT (Senior Peoples' Resources in North Toronto Inc.) has been providing services to help older adults (55-plus) and adults with disabilities live at home. Through them, you can purchase a range of services that are provided by SPRINT or a partner organization, from grocery shopping trips to counselling, from foot care to respite care. The organization offers community dining at eight locations in North Toronto, as well as exercise classes, discussion groups, and special events at seven locations, including services for the LGBT communities. Fees are currently around $21 per day for adult day programs, $15 per hour for in-home services, and $6 for a ride of up to 5 kilometres (less if you're going to a SPRINT program). You can get a hot meal delivered to your home for $5.75. The non-profit organization currently has 180 staff and 400 volunteers. A volunteer board of directors accountable to the local membership governs the organization, and its programs and services have evolved over the years to meet the changing needs of older adults and seniors in the community.[3]

We'll need an organization like SPRINT in our community, and we're going to want the services they provide to be broad-based and adapted to our needs. Even if someone plows our driveway, picks up our groceries, or helps us with the laundry, there will be a big hole in our lives without social engagement, mental stimulation, opportunities to give back, and someone to hug. And what about the services offered in those New York City senior centres referred to earlier, the underwater photography courses, organic and vegetarian meals, rooftop gardening, swimming, technology courses, and video conferencing? To provide ourselves with a holistic program addressing the full spectrum of our interests and needs, we'll need to get creative. To do that, we'll probably need to get involved, and there is a range of organizational models for us to consider.

The NORC Aging in Place Initiative is one of the earliest examples of a community-based comprehensive program to help people live in their own homes. Initiated in the mid-1980s by the UJA Federation of Jewish Philanthropies of New York City, the project brings health and social services to vulnerable seniors living in apartment buildings. NORC stands for a Naturally Occurring Retirement Community, such as those buildings in New York City where older adults are the predominant residents. What is significant about the Initiative is its emphasis on community building as a critical component of healthy aging and independence. Education, socialization, and recreational activities are key elements of the programs, as well as volunteer opportunities for program participants. Participants are provided with social work services, and offered health care management and prevention programs. The emphasis is on consumer choice and engagement, and NORC residents are seen as an essential part of program development and in voluntary capacities. Their website (www.norcs.org) provides resources to support other projects for community-based aging in place, and, to date, the NORC Aging in Place Initiative has been rolled out to 45 communities in 26 states.

If you're living in a NORC that is populated by lots of skilled and energetic residents, you may be able to self-organize to provide services to yourself and other seniors. This was the case for Beacon Hill Village, which was founded in 1999 by a group of long-time residents in this Boston neighbourhood who wanted to stay in their homes as they aged. As the founders explain, "We wanted to be active, taking care of ourselves and each other rather than being 'taken care of.'" To meet this goal, they developed a membership organization by and for people over the age of 50 that is funded by membership fees and donations. The organization operates with a paid staff, volunteers, and a variety of service providers and strategic partners. Membership benefits include social and cultural programs, transportation, referral services, a volunteer to assist you in your home or around town, and discounted home health care providers and health and wellness programs. In 2012, the organization had 400 members. From their website (www.beaconhillvillage.org), you can order a copy of the *Founders' Manual*, which describes their experiences in a "hands-on, tell-all style."[4]

To inspire other communities to self-organize, Beacon Hill Village has co-sponsored the Village-to-Village Network. These Villages are membership-driven, grass-roots organizations run by volunteers and paid staff. They coordinate access to affordable services including transportation, health and wellness programs, home repairs, social and educational activities and trips, and offer connections to screened discounted providers. The mission of the VtV Network is to enable communities to establish and manage their own aging-in-place organizations. Their website (www. vtvnetwork.org) offers webinars, how-to videos, discussion forums, and opportunities to share documents. Currently more than 70 Villages have been set up across the United States and in other parts of the world.

You may be inspired by the Village concept but feel that your community lacks the wherewithal to go it alone and set up a new organization. This was the conclusion of a group of people who wanted to bring services to Dakota County, West St. Paul, Minnesota. They liked the idea of a one-stop membership organization where a single phone call would connect seniors with the resources they needed to age in place. But their objective was to serve elders at all income levels, in a location that was more suburban than Beacon Hill Village. The group was willing to provide leadership, but concluded they needed to operate under the umbrella of an existing organization. They identified DARTS, a non-profit provider of transportation services, and convinced the organization to extend its mandate. The expanded DARTS (www.darts1.org/) is volunteer-based and offers help with basic household chores, resources and education for caregivers, ride services that help people get to work, go shopping, seek health care, and socialize, an information hotline connecting people with volunteers, resources, and organizations that can meet their needs, as well as education for families on eldercare issues. To give you a sense of the scale of the organization, DARTS announced at the end of 2010 that a government grant would enable them to provide 235 older neighbours with homemaking service, 75 with assistance with spring and fall yard work, 44 with snow removal, and 55 with help with lawn care.[5]

In his book *Elderburbia*, Philip Stafford, director of the Center on Aging and Community at Indiana University, concludes that these service co-operative models have much to recommend them. The approach increases awareness of available services, and confronts their fragmented nature and often demeaning admissions procedures. As well, the model addresses the problem that many services are only available to low-income seniors, leaving middle-income earners to fend for themselves. When it comes to program offerings, Stafford recommends a holistic approach. He suggests that the service mix strike a careful balance "which blends life-enhancing programs with down to earth, practical, concrete forms of assistance, thus reflecting what is perhaps the truth about aging, that it *is* a bed of roses, but with a few thorns thrown in."[6]

The Maine Approach, with its headquarters in Damariscotta, Lincoln County, is another creative approach to supporting aging in place. If Beacon Hill Village is a NORC, then the county of Lincoln and the state of Maine are rapidly becoming a NORCC (Naturally Occurring Retirement

Community County) and a NORCS (Naturally Occurring Retirement Community State), respectively. According to the 2010 census, Maine, with 15.9 per cent of the population over 65, is the third "oldest" state after Florida and West Virginia. In Lincoln County, one in five people is over the age of 65, making it one of the oldest counties in the country. Dr. Allan Teel developed the Maine Approach after spending decades as a medical practitioner in hospitals, nursing homes, and assisted living homes, and concluding that the better solution was assisting seniors to stay in their own homes. The Maine Approach uses technology for social networking and life management with a strong emphasis on volunteerism and the inclusion of elders themselves as an untapped volunteer resource. In his book, *Alone and Invisible No More: How Grassroots Community Action and 21st Century Technologies Can Empower Elders to Stay in Their Homes and Lead Healthier, Happier Lives,* Teel says the secret is helping elder clients find a way to help other elders. "Elder to elder, call it E2E if you like," he writes. "And when it is blended with the right amount of high tech, organization, family, neighbors, and only as much skilled medical care as necessary, the results can be amazing."[7] One of the techniques used by the Maine Approach for encouraging peer-to-peer contact is through an online social network. The network shares participants' photos, writings, and video clips, supplemented with video content from community events, speakers, and musicians.

Technological advancements in social networking will help us get the community support we need as we age. Tools such as meetup.com will reduce our isolation by facilitating connections with groups getting together for activities such as ballroom dancing, bridge, book clubs, and local park outings. Groups announce where they're gathering and at what time, and the pressure is off because you only join if you're willing and able, with no RSVP requirements. Social media tools are also an excellent resource for coordinating and sustaining care teams. Many of us have been part of a network using simple tools such as e-mail and Facebook to support a friend through a medical crisis or a family through an emergency. Some newer tools are tailor-made for care teams. CarePages (www.carepages.com) supports free patient blogs that connect friends and family during a health challenge. A designated person becomes the website manager and posts updates about the patient's condition, including requests for support. Friends and members of the care team post replies and supportive messages. You can restrict access to the site to designated participants and post private messages that only the website manager is able to view. E-mail alerts can let you know whenever a new update is posted. Ursula has been part of several teams that have been coordinated through CarePages and she has found the service invaluable. "I can't imagine the amount of time it would have taken to keep everyone updated and match people with assignments without this service. As well, there's another important function that's less tangible. The website allows people to see the full picture so they can appreciate that their contribution is valued and necessary. But they also understand that they are one among many volunteers and the demands on them needn't be overwhelming."

For a subscription fee, Tyze (www.tyze.com) allows you to coordinate a personal support team through a private, closed network. Friends, family, and caregivers can access a calendar and a "to-do" list to allocate and share tasks, and post pictures and stories to update medical conditions and celebrate successes. A "vault" with controlled access permits financial advisors and medical practitioners to retrieve and share financial documents or medical records. To illustrate the way technology can link you to your supporters, Tyze offers this quote from a man caring for his wife who has Alzheimer's. "It used to be so hard to ask for help. Now I put out a request and my network members are eager to lend a hand."

Many of these approaches to senior support rely on volunteers, and recruiting and retaining volunteers is always a challenge for non-profit organizations. The following groups are having some success by focusing on the needs of the volunteers as well as the seniors who are receiving the care. For example, SAIL (Supporting Active Independent Lives, www.sailtoday.org) is a non-profit organization providing resources to people 55-plus who reside in Madison, Wisconsin, and want to remain in their own homes. For an annual membership fee, SAIL provides referrals to pre-screened vendors, a daily check-in service, house checks, wellness services, and social events and clubs. To provide members with personal health coaching, they have partnering with university pharmacy students who are supervised by a geriatrics pharmacist and gain valuable experience.

Similarly, the Good Gym, based in East London, UK, focuses on the volunteers by encouraging runners to visit a senior as part of their weekly run, providing them with a purposeful destination. To emphasize the two-way nature of the relationship, the seniors are called "coaches" and each runner is partnered with his or her own "coach." The Good Gym website (www.goodgym.org) includes stories describing some of the relationships that have formed. For example, Harriet has been running to see her coach, Michael, every week for over a year. She brings the paper, they have a chat and sometimes she helps him with tasks such as filling out forms. Harriet doesn't live near her grandmother and appreciates the chance to hang out with an older person. She says, "Running can be mindless. It's great to have a sense of purpose. . . . I'm committed to him and the running is a by-product. I do it even if I don't have time to run. It feels like I'm making a difference."

At 80, Phil is hoping someone will take the initiative in his small community to improve services for seniors because he's determined to stay put. A full quarter of the population is over 65, and since housing stock is limited and most people he knows want to stay, the percentage of seniors will only increase. Phil feels services will have to get better. He is familiar with NORCs and the Beacon Hill Village model discussed above and thinks a similar approach could work in his community. "Let's say we set a subscription fee of $300 per year per senior household. With the hundred or so senior households, we could raise enough money to pay a coordinator $30,000 per year to keep all the pieces in place.

Following the model of the NORCs, the needs addressed would be multi-faceted: rides, companionship, chopping wood. And we'd set reasonable rates for services."

A ride service would really improve Phil's ability to age in place. He has recently been diagnosed with pulmonary fibrosis and a side effect of the prescribed drugs is reduced ability to focus, so he's reluctant to drive. Since few services are within walking distance of his home, he's dependent on others to get around. Fortunately, his wife still drives but were this to change, he'd be stuck. "Without improved transportation," Phil concedes, "if my wife and I lost our mobility, we'd be forced to leave." The community has a small number of spaces for assisted living in a facility with rent geared to income, but there's a waiting list. "But, like most of my friends, we want to live in our own home," Phil says, "and with a bit more support we could. Our health care is surprisingly good thanks to a clinic with doctors who rotate on two-to-three-week-long assignments. And I'm allocated 16 hours of home care support per month. I even get to request my preferred caregiver—he's an artist who works on huge canvases. Community is one of those things we take for granted until we need help."

If we were to learn from Phil's example, we would start implementing some form of community support now, so that it's in place when we need it. If programs already exist in our community, we could volunteer and help shape the services to address our needs. Either way, we'll feel good down the road when we're on the receiving end.

Homesharing

HOMESHARING has been used by seniors through the ages as a way of generating income or splitting expenses while receiving some support with daily living. Sometimes the seniors are the homesharers, other times they are the homeseekers looking for compatible, economical places to live. Some seniors open their homes to others primarily to share living expenses, others are seeking companionship. Some work through organizations that match them with partners, others are comfortable finding their own housemate(s). Some seniors have an ongoing relationship with an organization that supplies a rotating supply of housemates, such as an educational institution looking for student accommodation. Others feel comfortable advertising for their own housemates using websites such as Craigslist, Kijiji, and Easyroommate (http://ca.easyroommate.com). In this section we focus on sharing your living space with people to whom you are not related. However, some of the resources we discuss could help you negotiate shared space with your near and dear ones, which is the next topic.

Formal homeshare projects for seniors have been operating for decades and their success has been well documented. In 2000, researchers interviewed 252 homeowners in three midwestern US cities about their satisfaction with intergenerational homesharing. Older homeowners (70-plus) were more likely to be looking for companionship and assistance, and they reported significantly greater satisfaction than younger homeowners in the dimensions of health, well-being, and social activities. For younger homeowners (ages 50 to 69) the collection of rent was a priority and they emphasized the financial benefits from homesharing.[1] For more anecdotal evidence you can read or watch personal testimonials on the various websites that match homeshare participants. Let's Share Housing coordinates homeshares in the Portland, Oregon, area. Their website (www.letsshare housing.com) has a video interview with Dave, a senior who moved in with a married couple, both of whom are also seniors. This homeshare allowed Dave to meet his goal of moving into a home where he could integrate with a family. "I was being fairly particular," he says. "I wanted to be fairly involved with whomever it was, not just renting a room. I'd be able to share meals with them and perhaps do some of the cooking. And we'd be having conversations and we'd be interacting in several ways. It's really worked out well."

Calgary HomeShare, run by the Calgary Seniors' Resource Society (www.calgaryseniors.org), matches senior homeowners with adult homeseekers. The homeseekers provide 4 to 10 hours per week of help around the house in exchange for affordable accommodation. Rather than paying rent, the housemates make a pre-arranged financial contribute to offset utilities and other household costs, generally less than $400 per month. Their household tasks could include help with housework, gardening, snow removal, grocery shopping, and computer skills. Both parties fill out questionnaires to establish their needs and determine compatibility and are then interviewed by HomeShare staff. The homeowner is expected to provide a safe, clean environment, and the homeseeker provides a criminal record check, character references, and a security deposit. Calgary HomeShare facilitates the matchmaking and can help the parties negotiate the agreement and mediate the relationship. The goal is that both parties will benefit from the company and security of one another's presence, and seniors will be able to stay in their home through access to affordable support. Calgary HomeShare manager Cheryl Snider would welcome interest from people wanting to start a homeshare program in their own community. "We would be pleased to mentor them, share our materials, and discuss our learnings with them," she says. "Because the program is still relatively new, we are learning new things at each stage of growth and are constantly updating our materials and approaches. New programs have opened up in Red Deer, Alberta, and St John's, Newfoundland, and we have started www.home sharecanada.org to let people know about programs in Canada and how to contact them."[2]

If you decide to set up a homeshare matching service in your community, you will be able to draw upon a wealth of resources in addition to the Calgary HomeShare experience. The *Shared Housing Manual for Match-up Program* was written to help organizations set up their own match-up program and covers program design, staffing, record keeping, successful matchmaking, funding, and sample program forms. It can be ordered through the National Shared Housing Resource Center (NSHRC) (www.nationalshared housing.org), a clearinghouse of information for people looking to find a shared housing organization in their community or to help get a program started. Although the focus is on shared housing programs in the US, the resources have broader applicability. Members receive the *Shared Housing Newsletter*, which covers trends in homesharing as well as marketing and fundraising ideas. Another resource is Homeshare International, a charitable organization founded in London, UK, in 1999 to forge links between homeshare programs in eight countries and to stimulate the development of new programs. They share resources through their website (http://homeshare.org) and hold an international congress.

If you want to arrange your own homesharing, whether as homesharer or homeseeker, there are a variety of resources to help you. The website Caring.com has *Arranging Home Share: How to Help Your Loved Ones Find a Housemate* that includes tips on locating the housemate, figuring out your needs around income, help with chores and companionship, and checking out the renter's references.[3] The guide includes a list of questions for you to ask the prospective housemate to give you some insight into their habits and lifestyle. There are tips for what to include in your home-sharing agreement, how to prepare your home to ensure your own privacy and security, and advice on settling in and adjusting. Before you proceed with homesharing, it is essential to understand the relevant landlord/tenant laws in your jurisdiction. If you own a condo or are a tenant yourself, you need to understand those legal restrictions and obligations, as well. The website apartmentguide.ca, which provides a service for Vancouver-area renters and apartment owners, includes a section offering expert advice. Although the legal advice is specific to that city, you get a good overview of the issues you need to consider.

When Jean's marriage was on the rocks she decided to move in with Ned, a friend from her youth who had inherited a heritage home from his mother and was renting out rooms. That was several years ago. She's now 70 years old and has no plans to leave. In fact, she's upgraded her room, moving into a larger space that became available when another tenant died. She pays a monthly rent to Ned that includes charges for cable and phone. The real bonus for her is the arrangement around meals. "Ned does all the cooking," she explains. "I haven't cooked for two and a half years. He buys all the food in the house and keeps receipts and charges us accordingly. What I really love is that wonderful people are always dropping in for dinner and you never know who will be eating with us. Ned loves hosting and cooks dinner for whomever is there." For Jean, the key to their arrangement is its flexibility. "Things are always changing," she explains, "and what works about this place is its easy-going nature. I said to Ned, 'Since you're cooking, I'll clean.' He replied, 'If you feel like cooking cook, if you feel like cleaning clean, if you feel like working in the garden do that.' And so far, it's been working." For Jean, the other key to success is having a break from time to time. "I do house-sitting, so that helps whenever I feel impatient or hemmed-in. I just house-sat for three weeks, and another time it was for two whole months. And I go off on occasional trips to visit friends and family."

However, Jean has noticed that when new people are introduced into the mix, things don't run as smoothly. "Ned has allowed a teenager and her boyfriend to stay in the garage until they find their own space," she explains. "They are young and make a lot of noise and are always taking over the living room and making a fire and using the room as their own. There are unwritten rules about respecting everybody's space—rules they don't 'get.' The rest of us understand these rules, but Ned is too kind to say anything. Fortunately, they should be moving out soon."

Ned, Jean's landlord, is 63 and very conscious of the importance of his role in the house. "In all communities, someone has to do the job of providing," he says. "Whoever owns the place takes ownership of the community. It's a question of obligation. There are invisible tasks to be done and, in this community, either I do it or we hire someone, and for that we would need more resources." One of the problems with Ned's role is being tied to the property. "My plan was to live in France for a year but that can't happen now. I had a tenant that I could have left in charge, but he died. And, although I own the property jointly with my brother, he goes squirrelly after he has been here for a few days. So it's up to me to make the difference, no matter what. Even moving out wouldn't free me of the obligation." Ned has been pondering the future of the house. "I've been looking at statistics for our area that forecast yearly increases in taxes and cost of living and realize we're not going to have enough money," he says. "So, as we go into the future, we're going to need a more exact plan with an economic basis. It may mean changing the concept from this being *my* house and my brother's to *their* house. For example, if this house were to be organized more as a collective, the garden would become more important as a source of food. And, as we enter old age, we have to figure out who has to take care of whom." But Ned is conscious that what they are creating in his house is about more than economics and obligations. "You have to have something spiritual to recognize you are a community," he explains. "So when we have an occasion to celebrate we seize it. By celebrating, we have something we share, and people have something to feel a part of. We are battered veterans of life."

If you are participating in a landlord/tenant homesharing situation such as Ned and Jean's, you will need to comply with local regulations about the use of your property for rental purposes, and understand the legal implications of the arrangement. On its website, CMHC has information on tenant and landlord rights, responsibilities, and rental practices across the country, including fact sheets for each province and territory.[4]

At age 86, Geoffrey has been sharing his three-storey century home with students for decades. Although it's brought many rewards, he wouldn't recommend it as a strategy to support aging in place. "My demands on my students are very limited," he explains, "and I can't imagine having to count on them for regular duties. Most of them have been graduate students and, over the years, the academic pressures have really increased. Years ago I'd have four or five students and they'd take turns making dinner for everyone, and I'd roast a chicken on Sundays. Back then, it was more of a community. But that was before the university introduced evening classes. Right now I have two students and they are in very competitive programs and their hours are crazy. One of them is working on his PhD in chemistry and that involves working nights in the lab. The other student often works nights too. So I don't see much of them." For Geoffrey, the motivation to share his home was an altruistic one, and he has been repaid with enriching life experiences. "I've opened my home to students as a gift to them," he says. "This is my contribution. Most of them have been international students, who tend not to have much money. I don't want to see them thrown onto the expensive rental market, and even the residences are too costly for them. So I charge them a nominal $300 per month. But it's given me wonderful opportunities to visit former students in places like Madagascar and Prague. A number of them have kept in touch with me from all over the world and, recently, a student from Indonesia brought his new wife to visit me. Those students who are appreciative are very appreciative."

Geoffrey lays down a few basic rules and only rarely has he asked a student to leave. "We have no landlord/tenant agreement," he explains, "but there is a list of rules by which they have to abide. For example, nobody is to use the kitchen after 10 p.m. because my bedroom is overhead. They have to clean up the kitchen after themselves and keep their own rooms clean, as well as the upstairs bathroom. They can bring their friends over and entertain here, but they have to clear it with me beforehand. And they have to get along with each other, and with me. One of my students is very reliable—he's in charge of putting out the garbage and never fails to get it out. The other one cuts the grass sporadically and is supposed to help out with the gardening but I do most of the gardening with some help from a gardening service. The big problem with students is you have to work with their schedules. When I'm ready to do something they're just not around. Like snow shovelling. They'll do the shovelling but not before 9 a.m., which is when I need to have it done. I have a cleaning woman who comes once a week, so they really don't have to do much. I don't expect them to support me in my home and, fortunately, I don't need them to do that."

He warns that if you're going to try to find your own homesharers, the process can be onerous. "I work through the university housing services. Years ago they would advertise the rooms by posting notices up on the wall, but now they circulate the notices through the Internet and I get hundreds of applications. It's very time consuming to deal with the endless e-mails and go through the interview process. Based on the e-mails, I choose some students to interview by phone and then decide whether to interview them face to face. It's a pain in the neck, and I'm not getting any more patient as the years go by." Geoffrey is determined to stay in his home but doesn't see the students as part of the equation. "If something happens to me," he says, "I'll move my bedroom to the ground floor and hire help, although it won't be ideal because I only have a toilet on the ground floor—no bath or shower. If all else fails, I suppose I'll move to a retirement home. My friends have moved into several different ones and like where they are. But none of them are around here and I don't want to leave my neighbourhood. I tell everyone, 'They'll have to carry me out.'"

If you're interested in a shorter-term approach to companionship and income generation than homesharing, you may want to explore renting space to short-term guests. A number of online services such as HomeAway (www.home away.com) and Airbnb (www.airbnb.com) match hosts with paying guests who are seeking an alternative to a hotel. Hosts rent everything from a spare room to an apartment to an entire house, and may or may not be at home during the guest's stay. As a host you set your reservation requirements, establish your house rules, and can request a security deposit.

Communication and financial transactions between the parties take place on the website. The sites do not screen hosts or guests, but onsite reviews help you get to know other users, and hosts can reject a guest booking for any reason. As well as pocketing some additional income, you might make far-flung friends. At the time of writing, Airbnb included 70,000 accommodations in 19,732 cities in 192 countries, and the listings are translated into 7 languages. Ron Lieber reviewed Airbnb's offerings in New York City from a guest's point of view and reported mixed results. He encountered a host who was tipsy and another in revealing pajamas, and he suspects three of his five hosts were breaking a New York City law prohibiting people in residential buildings with three or more units from renting out the entire apartment for short-term stays. He admits that both hosts and guests might feel some security concerns about the set-up and reports that Airbnb badly handled a situation where a host returned to find that her home had been ransacked.[5] Airbnb has booked more than two million nights of lodging since 2008, so many people are taking the risk. If you want to become an Airbnb host, Lieber's experience highlights the importance of confirming the legality of your situation. My friend was keen on becoming a host in order to meet new people and earn some extra money until she read the details of her rental agreement, which expressly prohibited subletting.

Sharing Space with Children

SHARING A HOME with one's adult child may not be for everyone, but the strategy can be successful in supporting either senior or offspring, or both. The arrangement can take many forms: two generations may invest jointly in a property, the seniors may reside in their children's home, the children may reside in their parents' home, or the elder(s) may live in a "garden suite"—a free-standing structure built on the children's property, or vice versa.

Two years ago, Cliff's wife died of cancer. During the period that his wife had been receiving palliative care, the two of them had moved out of their apartment and into the home of their daughter and her family. After his wife's death, Cliff decided to stay on with his daughter's family, paying half the rent and doing chores. His older daughter, Claudia, was watching from the sidelines. "With four small children, it wasn't an ideal household," she observed. "It was also where his wife had died. But Dad stayed, partly from a fear of moving on, coupled with a feeling that he could help out my sister. If my brother-in-law hadn't become verbally abusive to him, he might still be there. But as soon as the problems started, my father packed his bags and moved in with my other sister and her family in another town." Claudia feels this new arrangement is much better for her father because the children in this household are teenagers and there are fewer demands on him. In addition, his rent is much cheaper. The new town is much easier to get around and he's made friends and found work as a handyman.

Sharing space with your children is emotionally fraught. "Some offspring have an expectation of how their parent should behave," Claudia says. "There's a tendency to infantilize and parent our parents and tell them how they should live. Although my dad is 77, he is very young for his age and doesn't see himself as old. He dropped into the seniors club but quickly left, saying it was full of white hair. He loves his freedom, and in his new location he doesn't have to wait by the phone. He's out and about all the time and has lots of lady friends. He can join the family for dinner, or not; he just has to let them know. There are no demands, nor hurt feelings, and no small children to mind."

But Claudia sees the issue from her sister's side, as well. "Your marriage has always been private, but when a parent moves in," she warns, "you give up your privacy. Both parties end up getting up close and personal, and privy to things they would normally have never known. There may be emotional instability with the adults or the children, and the issues may be on both sides." Having learned from her father's experience, she would caution against investing in a shared space with your offspring. "Hang on to your money," she advises. "You have to be free to move on if things don't work out. Contribute to food and pay rent for your space and let your children charge you a rent based on their improvements. But it's important for both parties that you keep your financing separate. It's not just the parent that may want to leave, the children may find out the parent is too difficult and want him/her to move out."

When families decide to homeshare, the Shared Housing Resource Center in Philadelphia stresses the importance of clarifying expectations. Their guide, *Homesharing for Families: A Self-Help Guide for Parents, Adult Children, and Other Relatives*, can be downloaded from their website and includes a self-questionnaire for both parties and a checklist of discussion points.[1] These tools can help you think through such issues as private versus shared space, division of household tasks, cleanliness standards, money matters (including utilities and food), living preferences around noise levels, smoking, entertaining, the length of the agreement, and many more issues. There is a model homesharing lease that can be used as the basis for a legal document once you've modified it for local laws. The Resource Centre has found that arrangements are only successful if they benefit both parties. They recommend establishing a trial period before jumping in with both feet and stress the importance of maintaining open and ongoing communication.

Policies and programs at every level of government can encourage families to live together. The government of Nova Scotia has a Parent Apartment Program which provides low-interest loans for additions or renovations to a single-family dwelling for the purpose of providing housing to a senior family member 50 years of age or older.[2] Japan has tax breaks to encourage multigenerational living arrangements and has promoted multigenerational mortgages, which offer low interest rates and typically last up to 50 years, and sometimes longer. In *Shock of Gray*, Ted Fishman reports that these practices have been successful in promoting multigenerational living, although not quite in the manner intended. The measures "were aimed at helping couples keep their parents with them at home, but in practice have provided great incentive for adult singles to stay in their parents' homes."[3]

In 2009, the city of Vancouver introduced zoning to permit laneway housing in some neighbourhoods, with the idea that the space could be a significant support for aging in place. Laneway housing is a detached dwelling, usually facing the back laneway where the garage is located, which cannot be sold separately from the main dwelling but can be rented out. The potential uses are multiple: seniors could downsize to the laneway housing from their main home and rent the main home as an income generator, or they could rent the smaller dwelling to caregivers. Children could build laneway housing for their aging parents or vice versa.

If you're interested in this option but face prohibitive zoning bylaws, it's useful to know that Canada Mortgage and Housing Corporation is recommending single-lot, laneway, infill housing to municipalities as a cost-effective way of meeting critical housing needs. To encourage municipalities to expand this form of housing, they have produced a research document that can be downloaded from their website.[4] In 2010, the city of Portland, Oregon, decided to waive system development charges for ADUs (accessory dwelling units: self-contained homes built on the same lot as a single-family home) and voted to increase the ADU size limits from one-third to three-quarters of the size of the main house. The result has been a boom in these units.[5]

About thirty years ago, Patricia and her daughter bought a triplex with a friend, and after twelve years, the two of them bought out the friend. Patricia is now 75 years old. She lives in the ground-floor apartment, her daughter and family live on the second floor, and they rent the third-floor apartment to Patricia's son and his family. Patricia's four grandchildren, ranging in age from 16 months to 18 years, live in the building. "None of us has any regrets," she says. "All three of us have completely autonomous apartments. We're not obligated to see each other just because we're sharing the building, but we're there to support one another. The key to our success is the possibility of complete autonomy." The other critical factor is the care they took with their legal agreement. "Any time you go into a business relationship with a family member or a friend," Patricia explains, "you put yourself at risk. We worked on our co-ownership contract for six months. We needed a simple and clear agreement so there wouldn't be any friction. And because one of the parties was my daughter, it was even more important. The agreement stipulated that when the third party wanted to sell he first had to offer it to us. When that time came each party got an estimate and the average was used to set the price. It was clear and straightforward and the proof of its success is that we remain good friends." Looking ahead, Patricia has no plans to move. "I plan on living here until I die. If I were physically incapacitated and had to use a wheelchair I would have to rearrange the corridors. But even in a wheelchair, I can still imagine living here. My son does all the repairs in exchange for reduced rent, so when I find it too difficult to get out of this bed, he can raise its level so I can get in and out more easily."

Despite her happiness with her arrangement, Patricia acknowledges that co-ownership with your children has its issues. "One of the dangers," she says, "is that the relationship you have with your children is more intimate and you have more knowledge of their day-to-day challenges. If, for example, you don't particularly like your daughter-in-law, then there is more potential for friction, so there has to be a basic liking. You have to work hard at not jeopardizing relationships, you need to have some self-control, and you need to be discreet. But there is always the possibility of privacy; you don't have to know everything. You also have to be able to say no. And you don't have to be a babysitter just because you're living in the same building. But I'll never have to worry about loneliness living here, and for old people, that is the biggest thing to overcome."

Another approach is to build from scratch with multi-generational use in mind. In this way, you can design spaces both for togetherness and for privacy. When her mother was finding it difficult to live alone at 87 years of age, Stephanie and her husband decided to build a new home that would be suitable for both generations. Stephanie and her husband are in their sixties, all three children have left the nest, and they were ready to downsize. They applied the proceeds from the combined sales of their own house and their mother's condo to the creation of a new home that would satisfy everyone's needs. The house, built from scratch on a residential street, includes a self-contained apartment for Stephanie's mother that was designed to allow her to live an independent but supported life. The mother's suite is located in a raised basement with nine-foot ceilings that opens onto its own private patio. It features a spacious sitting room and bedroom. "Mom was able to bring most of her living room furniture with her so I think that provides comfort," Stephanie says. "She doesn't have a fully-equipped kitchen, just a sink and counter with basic appliances, but that seems to be all she needs. As we age, it seems the hours of sleeping and awake become skewed, and coffee and toast at 4:00 a.m. is just what the doctor ordered!"

They have been living in the new space for the past year and Stephanie says that, for the most part, the arrangement is working well. "One area that needs some work," she says, "is adjusting our boundaries so that we get some privacy. What is difficult is that Mom has no social life of her own and is totally reliant on her family and me for interests. It's understandable because her two friends have passed away and her husband is in an extended care hospital with ALS. Mom visits him almost every day and his condition is worsening and that is adding great stress to Mom's days. So Mom eats upstairs with us most of the time and spends a lot of her days upstairs. I do sometimes feel that I need my own 'quiet time' and alone space. But we are slowly working that out. We got Mom a very affectionate cat and this has helped absorb some of her time and energy, of which she has plenty!"

Another issue to be considered with shared housing is what happens when the family travels. "At this point, Mom refuses any outside assistance if we are away," Stephanie says. "Her health is mediocre but she is fiercely independent and doesn't want to have 'strangers' around. So this is a worry. But, all in all, the plan is working well from our perspective so far. Mom is enjoying the new house. It is full of sunshine and light and the new gardens are lovely and I think she is feeling more and more at home."

In another example from Mill Valley, California, it was the grandparents who took the lead to build a home with their daughter and her two sons. Their son and his family were already living in another home on the same property and the grandparents' goal was to see a lot more of their grandchildren. The design of the new house joins two separate living spaces with a living roof and has individual entrances for both families. The grandparents occupy the top storey. Features to allow them to age in place include an elevator, wall blocking for bathroom grab bars, accessible hardware, and a foot pedal for the kitchen sink. Living so close to their grandchildren provides opportunities for lots of everyday contact when they drop in to say hi or wave as they head off somewhere. The grandfather says moments like these "make all the extra effort involved in building this house worth it."[6]

In *Unassisted Living: Ageless Homes for Later Life*, Chapman and Rosenfeld include the layout and photos for a home built on a Wyoming ranch that had been in the owner's family for three generations. Visiting children are accommodated in living quarters in an adjacent barn. The plan is to reverse positions down the road, with the parents occupying the smaller space in the barn and the children moving into the main house.

This Wyoming ranch solution is similar to what Sheryl has in mind. When she got married she moved with her husband to his family's farm where they raised two children. Her in-laws owned the farm and lived in another building on the property. She is now 71 years old and has been a widow for over twenty years and still lives on the farm. They have 146 acres. They rent out about 90 acres and farm the rest with beef cattle, wheat, and barley. Sheryl supported her mother-in-law to stay on the farm and sees herself repeating this pattern. "After my father-in-law died," Sheryl explained, "I made an agreement with my mother-in-law that she could live on the property until her death and I would take care of her. As it turned out, she lived there another eight years but her care needs were such that she had to spend her last few years in a nursing home." After her mother-in-law left her home, Sheryl renovated the building and turned it into a rental property. In the short term, she wants the extra income, but down the road she sees it as a retirement property for herself. "I own half the farm with the other half divided 80/20 between my son and daughter. My son has the larger share because he's been putting money into the farm. I've been putting money into the house. The idea is that my son will move into the family home and I will own the house 50/50 with him and he will pick up the house expenses. Eventually I'll move into my former in-laws' property. But in the short term, I have a new boyfriend and we're thinking of moving in together and this would mean moving to another town where he lives. So we'll see what happens with my long-term plan."

These examples of sharing space with our children presume relatively healthy seniors, but what happens if we develop disabilities and can no longer care for ourselves? This is where many of us draw the line, saying, "I don't want to be a burden on my children." But if we organize things well, we may be able to help our offspring achieve their goals, while meeting our own needs. Noreen's 93-year-old mother has advanced dementia. Her husband had been her principal caregiver and after he died she expressed her wish to live with her family. Because she and her husband had lived frugally, their savings were sufficient for her children to put in place a care program that works for everyone. "My brother bought a bigger house with a suite on the ground floor," Noreen explains. "He charges Mom $1,000 per month rent, which contributes to his mortgage. Her money also provided some bridge financing, which he repaid. The house is a bungalow on a hill on a huge lot and the suite has a walkout to a patio with full-on sun. So it's a lovely place for Mom to live. Her caregiver lives in another room on the same floor. She works weekdays and we hire additional caregivers for the weekend. My brother visits with Mom first thing in the morning and gets up at night if she needs him. He uses two types of monitors—a baby monitor that captures noise and a motion detector that tells if she gets out of bed. Three days a week she goes on a bus to a social club and a caregiver takes her out for lunch after the club, and she goes out for a walk every day. This has been on-going for two years now, and although my mother's mental capacity is declining, her physical health is improving." But Noreen emphasizes that to run an operation like this costs a lot of money. "It's a $100,000-per-year operation to care for my mother," she says. "But the benefits are enormous—for everyone. From my brother's perspective, this approach has allowed him to buy a much bigger house. But more importantly, being able to care for my mother in this way has enhanced his life. And the quality of her care gives both of us great peace of mind."

Nola modified her house so that her mother, Judy, could live with her after she broke her hip at age 86. Nola is the eldest of Judy's four children and when Judy said, "I'd like to live with one of my kids," Nola proposed her home. "We had the room and Mom had a comfort level with me,"

Nola explains. "And location was important. We lived in the city, unlike my siblings, and Mom was able to maintain her connection to her church." Nola used her share of the projected inheritance from her mother's estate to pay for an addition to her home that contained a large one-room suite with bathroom and ramp access. "Having her own suite gave Mom a place where people could come and visit, but they didn't have to be with her the whole time, and she didn't have to be with them. She got to see a lot of my children so that made her life much more interesting. Mom wanted to be in charge of her own space. She washed her own dishes until the last few years and counted out her own pills. Both tasks took her a very long time and she would laugh about it, but did not want to give up these responsibilities. We decided not to put in an oven, only a microwave, and for the first two years she did miss having an oven. After that she wouldn't have been able to use it anyway. We also put in a small galley sink and she missed a bigger sink. That probably was a mistake."

After living with Nola for two years, Judy developed a stress fracture and the caregiving intensified. The caregiving was supposed to be a bit more shared among the family members, but as often happens, that didn't pan out. "It comes down to a question of who steps up to the plate, and one person ultimately assumes responsibility," Nola says. "But my sister talked on the phone with Mom nearly every day, and that was a really important connection for both of them. And my brother provided financial support. And

Mom also had her own money, so this allowed us to provide her with a high level of companionship. As she got weaker, we needed someone with professional skills to assist her, which cost about $30,000 to $40,000 per year. Mom contributed $200 per month for her household expenses, which was then raised to $500 per month."

Then, life threw Nola another curve ball. Three years after her mother moved in, her husband had a severely debilitating stroke. "I felt like I was running a retirement home," Nola says. "When Mom first moved in we ate separately because I didn't want us to be tied down to her schedule, and we didn't always share her taste in food. But after my husband's stroke we all ate together and neither of them could express what they wanted to say. All through his rehab, my husband gravitated to Mom. He loved spending time with her. Even if he couldn't talk he could listen. They laughed together and provided community for each other. And because I had all the caregivers coming in already for Mom, I was able to lead my own life. After Mom's death it was harder because my husband needed my company. A few years after Mom's death, my husband died."

Nola is 70 years old and I ask her how the extraordinary level of caregiving she provided to her mother and husband has affected her choices for her own future. "I was very glad to be able to do this for my mother," Nola said, "but it wasn't always easy. Although I had some support from my family, I looked after all the logistics. If I hadn't had access to money it would have been a very different story, but I still had the anxiety and most of the organizing. As for me, I have a condo ready and waiting for my downsizing. I wouldn't want to live with any of my children."

If you decide to co-invest with your children, it is important to think through the financial implications of your decision. Since your flat or laneway house or co-joined residence cannot be sold separately from the rest of the property, it might not be easy to get your investment back if things don't work out. The problem is well illustrated by a story I was told about a woman who sold her house to her daughter and son-in-law and used the proceeds to renovate the house to include a granny flat where she would live. But she was essentially sharing the house with her kids. Then she had a fight with them. The main issue was her feeling that her son-in-law was not pulling his weight; she couldn't stand to watch her daughter doing way more than her share. Her daughter's response was that it was none of her mother's business. When it became apparent that the threesome wasn't going to work out, the woman moved out. They subsequently made up but continue to live apart. The unanswered question is whether the woman ever recouped her financial investment.

Sharing Space with Other Family

SHARING A HOME with family other than offspring could provide some of the comforts of familiarity without the challenges of the parent/child relationship. Siblings may move in together in the latter part of their lives, spouses may separate but move into different parts of a house to give each other more space while still sharing expenses, and former partners may reconnect in new ways.

Alice and Judd are former partners. They're now 79 years of age. When they were in their fifties, they split up and moved into their own homes but continued to be friends. For four years, Alice ran a B&B in her house, and then she added a kitchen on the second floor so it could function as a rental unit. For Alice, this opened up the possibility of living again with Judd because they would each have their own space. "Judd was living in his own home and me in mine," she explains, "and finally I suggested, 'Why don't you live upstairs from me? You can help me with chores, but we'll make our own suppers.'" Alice finds lots of benefits in this "separate but together" arrangement. "It beats living together because it gives me a lot more choice over what I get to do. I can be with him or alone. I watch TV at his place and bring up my supper. If I need him in the middle of the night he can get there quickly enough, and the same goes for me reaching him. I can call him if I have something heavy to lift." Alice and Judd both contribute what money they have to cover their operating costs. "We can only afford this," she says, "because we're not big consumers. I've always been strong on living simply and have managed to do this for a long time. I find the most interesting things right under my feet. The secret is liking what you have." I ask Alice what the future holds. "If I become senile or too crippled I wouldn't want him to take care of me," she replies. "I also wouldn't want to be his personal caregiver, although I could do some things, like help him with his bath. If I need more care, I'll go into an assisted living place. Judd says he'll live here until he dies of a heart attack."

Rita is 77 years old and lives with Flora, who is a couple of years younger. Although they aren't officially blood relatives, Rita explains that they met when they were students and Rita's parents unofficially adopted her. "She is my 'sister by affection,'" Rita says. "This is a Chinese term. My parents fell in love with her and her children became their unofficial grandchildren. They were so close that, when my parents died, they came a great distance to their funerals." Rita and Flora have shared a duplex for the past eight years. "I live in the basement and she lives upstairs," Rita explains. "I have a self-contained apartment with my own entrance and my own washer and dryer. There is a door at the top of the stairs, but it's never shut. Flora's part has two floors, including an upper floor with two bedrooms and bathrooms. I'm quite well-off and Flora pays her share with what she can." Rita's mother died at 84 and her father at 94 and they were able to live in their own home except for the last two years of her father's life. "When my parents got old, having Flora and her family made it so much better, otherwise I would have been dealing with everything all by myself. All of them supported me, for which I am very grateful." Watching her parents age has made Flora conscious of her own aging. "You do need to think ahead," she says. "If we needed to, we could put an elevator on the stairs and live on the top floor. If we needed care, someone could live in and take care of us. And we have friends and some family who would support us."

After his second wife left him, the novelist Kingsley Amis shared a house with his first wife, Hilary, and her third husband. Decades earlier, Kingsley had left Hilary for wife number two. Their son, Martin Amis, takes credit, along with his older brother, for coming up with the idea for the housesharing. In his memoir, *Experience*, Martin writes that he and his brother proposed the idea to the principals because their father needed constant companionship after the collapse of his second marriage. The sons were motivated to come up with a solution because they were both in their early 30s and decided it was "a bit early, we felt, to commit our lives to Dadsitting—but we couldn't rule it out." The proposal also resolved another worry of Martin's.

Although his mother was happy in her third marriage, she and her husband and daughter wanted to move to London but couldn't afford the expensive city. As he says, "It was an unconventional proposal, true; but they were an unconventional crowd." Martin and his brother gave the experiment six months, maybe a year, but it lasted 15 years, until Kingsley's death. In the later years, Kingsley developed Alzheimer's and Hilary became his caregiver until he was sick enough to require nursing care. Martin includes descriptions of the challenges of her role, saying she was "exhaustively familiar with her ex-husband's scrapes and scares." From Martin's perspective, his mother brought Kingsley "back to life and love." As for Hilary, Martin felt that only the memory of love remained, but she was in it for the duration because "her conscience would permit nothing less." However, Martin's book includes a photo of his parents from that period and their pleasure in one another's company is visible.

These examples illustrate the value of flexibility and keeping an open mind when we consider our future options. A thick skin and the ability to ignore other people's critical opinions are also important. Martin says that when they came up with the housesharing idea "everyone else . . . considered the idea both bizarre and impracticable. 'Like an Iris Murdoch novel,' they kept saying."[1]

Downsizing

THERE ARE A VARIETY of motivators that push or pull people to downsize. One oft-cited goal is sparing our offspring the cleanup after we're gone. Irma articulates this sentiment when talking about her friend. "She's the Queen of Denial," she says. "Of the 16 of us who hang out together, she's the only one still living in a big house with stairs and stacks of stuff. I know her daughter will handle it, but it's not fair to do that to her. It's mean to leave your family with all that stuff."

Irma was 79 when she downsized to a 400-square-foot apartment on the 16th floor of a high-rise building that was closer to the centre of the city. She made the move after she developed an infection in her leg that made it difficult to go up and down the 29 stairs to her previous apartment. As she puts it, "I gave up a quirky historic condo for a cement high-rise shoe box." Now 82, she is delighted with her decision. "I get to watch the eagles," she says. "It's got everything I need. Every morning I swim 20 lengths in the swimming pool. I wanted a place where I could walk to everything or catch a bus because I have a 1993 car and knew it wouldn't last forever." Irma is planning on staying where she is, even were she to require more care. "I'll hire a physio and someone to clean the house. I can walk to the thrift stores and get to the seniors centre for classes. I'm part of a great group of friends and whenever one of us is sick someone will take over and organize people to bring what you need. When I had a medical problem a few months ago, I had a spate of chicken soup. As you degenerate, you need a circle of friends like this. So all in all, I could manage well here unless I were to become really incapacitated. The way I see it, I'll be here until they cart me out."

The desire to reduce the demands of running a large house and yet stay close to home has encouraged some aging urbanites to downsize to nearby condos. In Meredith's case, she and her husband got married when they were both in their sixties and they each had their own home, so they downsized from two houses into a condo. "We feel we would be able to live here well into our eighties," she explains. "If either of us were to become somewhat incapacitated, the condo could be retrofitted to accommodate such a situation. If we remain healthy and able, we could stay here into our nineties. My greatest hope is that we will make good decisions for ourselves as we see our circumstances change. I've been watching my aging parents, who are still in their home at ages 87 and 89. My dad is very frail and dependent on my mom, who is healthy, but tired." Meredith and her husband chose their downtown location to help them age in place. "I used to live in the suburbs," she says, "and I find the city has so much more to offer people of all ages. I've started taking courses and I'm meeting people in their late seventies who continue to enjoy learning, and by living where they do, they have the opportunity to do so. Should my husband predecease me, I am blessed with a wonderful circle of friends with whom I will share travel, reading, plays, and all manner of good things."

While some people, like Meredith, purchase condominiums, others move into rental apartments. There are pros and cons to each approach. At 71, Marcie has been living for many years in the same apartment in a small apartment building. There was a period of time when she would have raved about the wonderful community the tenants formed, but things have changed. "The problem with a rental space," she says, "is that people come and go. I used to have regular parties for my neighbours and friends because my neighbours were also my good friends. Then I gave it up because our building had lost all the good people. I recently gave a party, but it was my first in four years. Also, a rental space can be torn down. But I don't want to buy a condo. At this stage of my life, I don't want to own anything. I don't want the responsibility. My kids have suggested I might consider some sort of retirement setting. Depending on how it was structured, maybe there would be less turnover and more control over who were your neighbours."

A year ago, when she was 79, Shirley moved into an apartment building downtown and, so far, is very pleased with her decision. "After my husband died, I sold our house and moved downtown and made new friends," she says. "I had lost most of my previous friends. Some had died, and then there were the friends who dropped me after my husband died. So I moved into this apartment building and joined the community centre and got to know a completely new group of people. What I like about this building is that people of all ages live here—and you can open your windows, plus you have a balcony. The only problem with the building is there isn't a place for people to get together. But they organize events several times a year, around Christmas and a summer barbecue, and they hold events in the foyer if the weather isn't nice. I have no interest in moving into a retirement home. This is the first time in my life that I have lived alone and I like it. I like scrambling eggs at 11 p.m. at night if I feel like it, or doing whatever I feel like doing. I miss my husband, but I can't imagine that I'll ever want to live with someone else again."

Kathy and her husband have been living in a condo for the past four years and she has no regrets about selling their house. "But life as a condo owner is different," she explains. "It's a vertical community and the elevator gives you more intense contact with your neighbours than a curb. You don't necessarily have much in common with the other owners and you don't get to know them that well because your lives are lived elsewhere. But since your condo is one of your biggest investments, how they behave matters. What they contribute in terms of labour and finances to the condominium complex becomes important and, to protect your investment, you need to monitor your condo board carefully. I've been on the board for five years and chair for three. At 71 years of age, I'm one of the younger ones. But that's because our building was built in 1974 and people tend to buy and stay."

If we're looking to buy a condo, Kathy recommends that we look at buildings that have been around for a number of years, rather then buying into a complex that is yet to be built. We should read the condo minutes and talk to the neighbours and find out what we're getting into. On the other hand, she warns against buying in at a point when it's time for extensive repairs on an aging building. If the condo board hasn't established a reserve fund large enough to handle future maintenance and upkeep, we could be in trouble. Due diligence is required.

My friend Suzanne lived in a condo for over a decade and her advice echoes Kathy's. "Before signing on to buy a condo you must get a statement on the condo reserve fund. This is critical because the fund finances all major repairs, such as structural problems. For example, repairing a garage leak could turn out to be a very expensive endeavour. If there isn't ample money in the reserve fund, the individual owners are charged, and I heard of a situation where a condo owner opened his mail to find a bill for $20,000. You need to find out who is on the board and get a reading of how they conduct business. If there is a lot of conflict, it will impact the owners, so my advice would be to stay away. You need to find out about the management company hired by the board, and again, if that relationship is shaky, I would think twice. And speak to people in the condo, if you can, to get their impressions. As to size, I think there's a fine balance between the anomie of some of the large condos and the forced intimacy of the six-to-eight unit condos." CMHC has published a *Condominium Buyers' Guide* that identifies important questions to ask and has a checklist to narrow down the choice between different types of condominiums.[1]

The above examples are of people who downsized and stayed pretty close to home. Other people make a major move and relocate at the same time as they downsize. That's what Glenda and Dwight did when they sold their acreage and moved to the other end of the country to support family members struggling with illness. The couple had been living with Glenda's father on a large rural property where the labour of all three of them was required to handle the upkeep. When Glenda's father died, he left a large gap that was hard to fill. At the same time, Glenda's younger sister, who was living in another province, was coping with muscular dystrophy and a husband with Alzheimer's, and her condition began to deteriorate. Glenda and Dwight, who were both 69 years old at the time, decided to sell their property and relocate to be near their struggling family members and help out. Glenda's sister died about three months after they arrived and their brother-in-law died a year later. Glenda says, "We were so grateful we were able to be with them at the end. It made a big difference to their lives—and to ours."

Glenda and Dwight decided to remain in their new community. They are both 76 now and couldn't be happier with their accidental location. They live fairly close to one son and his family, which includes three grandsons, and they get to visit with them often. The town where they live has about

10,000 people with about 40 per cent of the population over the age of 65. "Having lots of older people means that our age group is catered to with excellent services," Glenda explains, "but there are lots of young people around. And the town is friendly and beautiful." They bought themselves a bungalow and although they have a lovely garden, it's small, and the amount of time they spend on home maintenance is dramatically reduced from their rural days. "We plan to stay in our home as long as we can," Glenda says, "even if it requires hiring a housekeeper. We have room in the basement for a live-in."

Designers and builders are coming up with ever more innovative ways to squeeze maximum livability from small spaces, so downsizing doesn't have to mean sacrificing convenience or beauty. A colleague of mine told her children that when she gets old she wants to live on their property in a Tumbleweed House. "That's all I'll need," she reassures them. The Tumbleweed Tiny House Company (www.tumbleweedhouses.com) offers both floor plans and pre-assembled houses that can be towed to your site. One of their tiny abodes is the 102-square-foot Weebee House. A feature of this house that may appeal to both my colleague and her children is the portability of the structure. Since it can be situated wherever you can park a travel trailer, she can move along if things get stale. But she'll need to keep her agility for this one; you use a built-in ladder to reach the queen-sized sleeping loft that has been slipped under the house's pitched roof.

Weebee House is one of thirty modular and prefab houses, all under 1,000 square feet, included in *Tiny Houses* by Mimi Zeiger. Zeiger is exploring the microgreen side of sustainable architecture and the international houses she profiles apply green living principles and use renewable resources for construction. Many of her examples employed off-site prefabrication to minimize ecological impact. Zeiger challenges us to take a look at our own homes and consider how much space we actually use.

In his book *Tiny Homes, Simple Shelter: Scaling Back in the 21st Century*, Lloyd Kahn goes even smaller to look at really tiny houses, under 500 square feet. His book features some 150 builders working around the world who are promoting downsizing and self-sufficiency with a rich variety of options including building your own, using a kit or prefab, or living in a movable shelter such as a bus or houseboat. The book also includes amenities you may wish to add for your next stage of life, including studios, saunas, garden sheds, and greenhouses. The book includes stories from the owner-builders who have decided to scale back and live with less stuff, as well as links to websites and plans for tiny houses.

In May 2012, the *New York Times* reported on the delivery of the first MEDCottage to a general practitioner who intended to house her mother in the backyard of her Virginia home. The 12-by-24-foot prefab house has sleeping, living, and bathing areas, with utilities and plumbing connected to the primary residence. The building uses technology to assist with caregiving duties, offering devices to monitor vital signs, alert caregivers to problems, and provide medication reminders. A MEDCottage can be purchased outright or leased, and the 2012 price for a new unit was US$85,000. Because of zoning restrictions, currently only about half the states in the US allow these units for a family member. Virginia state law permits temporary medical dwellings on a resident's property, assuming a physician validates the requirement and the unit is removed when it's no longer needed.[2]

Living smaller can be liberating. When Kathy and her husband downsized from their large home to a condo she found it exhilarating to work with less. "When you're in a small space you have to de-accession," she says. "I felt shiny and new-born. It's like the Zen story where the man collects one perfect object. This was an opportunity to completely rework my living space. I have seen people try to cram their old lives from large homes into small spaces and I don't think it works. I really felt like I was starting again." As well, Kathy likes the impact the new space is having on her relationship with her husband. "It's cosy, intimate, you become more attached to each other," she says. "We started out as a couple with not much, and now we're back to where we were. I like the arc. It brings back shared memories. As well, it gives us a sense of security knowing that if something happened to either of us, the remaining partner would be living in some degree of comfort and not have to handle the downsizing alone. I wouldn't want my husband to go through all that by himself." As for regrets about living in a smaller space, at first Kathy couldn't think of any. "Oh, there is one thing," she says. "I miss my barbecue."

Cohousing

COHOUSING is a relatively new way for seniors to house themselves that deserves a serious look. By combining privately owned homes or apartments with shared or commonly held property, seniors can gain both independent living and community support. Interest in cohousing is growing among Canadian seniors, with the first seniors cohousing complex opening in Saskatoon, several other senior projects under development, and seniors residing in several intergenerational cohousing communities. At first glance, cohousing seems to be another form of condominium or strata complex, but there is a critical difference. In a condominium, the shared property is managed by a condominium board and, although you want to assure yourself that your property is in good hands, the extent to which you actively participate is your choice. In contrast, with cohousing there is an expectation that the project will be community-driven and that, as a resident, you will be an active participant. At the building stage, the prospective residents participate in planning the complex with the design goal of facilitating a strong sense of community. This is encouraged by including shared property for amenities that may include common gathering spaces, a children's playroom, guest accommodations, as well as a garden, a workshop, and other amenities. Although each home will have its own kitchen, there is usually a common dining area and, possibly, a community kitchen. After the complex is up and running, residents are expected to provide shared leadership in its management, and participate, to some extent, in activities with their neighbours.

Denmark, Sweden, and the Netherlands are credited with the first cohousing projects, and the concept was introduced to North America with the publication in 1988 of *Cohousing: A Contemporary Approach to Housing Ourselves* by the husband-and-wife team of Katie McCamant and Charles Durrett. In 2009, Durrett published *The Senior Cohousing Handbook*, a comprehensive guide to joining or creating a seniors cohousing project. Since 1991, 127 cohousing communities have been completed in North America and another 118-plus are in various stages of development. The projects exhibit a great variety of ownership structures, organizing principles, community size, and design. While most are intergenerational projects, several have been designed as seniors cohousing, although they may not have age restrictions.

Silver Sage Village (www.silversagevillage.com), completed in 2007 in Boulder, Colorado, is one of five senior cohousing communities in the United States. The project consists of 16 duplexes and attached homes on a 0.7-acre property that includes a community centre and a common interior courtyard with sidewalks, flower beds, and a vegetable garden. The community centre incorporates a kitchen, dining area, two guest rooms, as well as crafts, media, exercise, and meditation rooms. Several units have been designated under affordability guidelines to ensure accessibility to lower-income individuals and families. Silver Sage was built by Wonderland Hill Development Company, one of the largest developers of cohousing in the US, and its president, Jim Leach, is one of its residents. Leach explains that residents at Silver Sage are expected to participate in the co-operative work of managing and maintaining the community, which is handled through monthly and team meetings. He shares meals twice a week with neighbours in the common house, and they frequently go to events together, sharing rides and shopping for one other. "Individual neighbours do many things that add value based on their interest and skills," he writes, "things like gardening, arts and crafts, and gourmet cooking for the community. This all makes us a closer connected group of neighbours. The diversity of interests, expertise, and energy for certain things makes it easier for us to experience the things that enrich our lives."[1] There are no restrictions on who can purchase a condo at Silver Sage, not even a minimum age. However, when Philip Stafford interviewed residents for his book *Elderburbia*, he was told that people who were not willing to engage in the level of participation required have been turned away.[2]

In Canada, the first seniors cohousing project opened in 2012 in Saskatoon. Wolf Willow was designed for adults

55 years of age and over, and comprises 21 apartment-style condominiums. Shared space includes a communal kitchen, laundry room, guest room, and music room, as well as the courtyard around which the residences are located. The property is within walking or biking distance to a farmer's market and the downtown, and is near a pedestrian/bike path. The project developed over a four-year period from the impetus of seven friends (four households). After two years it had grown to 25 individuals, 16 of whom were equity members. The rest were associate members who participated in the meetings as a way of becoming better acquainted with the people and the concept. The members hired a project manager who was an experienced cohousing professional and lived in cohousing herself, and they engaged an architect who had designed other cohousing complexes. By move-in, the project had reached 36 members. When member Eliza Meggs described the group's motivation, she made reference to *You Could Live a Long Time: Are You Ready?* and its concept of a Retirement Emotional Circle Plan (RECP). "The friends involved in Wolf Willow Cohousing are building their RECP," she wrote.[3] The Wolf Willow website (www.wolfwillowcohousing.ca) includes their mission statement and vision, as well as personal profiles of the members. Other seniors cohousing projects are underway in Sooke, Chilliwack, and Smithers, all in British Columbia.

Charles Durrett has been involved as designer or architect for many of the cohousing developments and finds that some seniors prefer the youthful energy of intergenerational housing, while others want senior cohousing that has been designed around their unique needs. For example, guest rooms in senior cohousing tend to be larger to accommodate visiting families or caregivers, and showers are built to accommodate wheelchairs. In *The Senior Cohousing Handbook*, Durrett talks about the challenge of setting age restrictions at the initial planning stage. He has found that secret ballots are used sometimes to come to a true consensus. In his experience, senior cohousing groups look for people over 50 who enjoy good health and will sometimes set an upper limit of 65 or 69 at move-in. "All the groups I interviewed agreed that it is best to stagger the ages of residents," he says, "erring toward younger people in the early days of the community when there is a lot of work to do."[4] In Wolf Willow, at the point of move-in, the residents ranged in age from the mid-fifties to 80.

The Canadian Cohousing Network (www.cohousing.ca) was formed in 1992 to make the process of creating a cohousing community easier and more economical by connecting people and sharing resources. Resources on their site include the video *Building Community with Cohousing*, which provides some insight into the cohousing experience from the point of view of several residents in three communities. A senior talks about the specific benefit she gains from living in an intergenerational cohousing community. "I am exceptionally lucky because my daughter and son-in-law and two grandchildren live here so that's a very special benefit for me." Two of the interviewees address a common worry that, given its emphasis on community, cohousing may mean a loss of privacy. "The biggest benefit is that if I want to be alone, I can be alone, and if I want company, I just walk downstairs," one resident says. Another talks about this issue when it comes to her and her husband. "Neither of us are extremely gregarious people but whenever we really want to go and talk to somebody, about something trifling or something serious, people are there."

Another issue addressed in the video is caregiving. "We don't have an expectation that we'll be taken care of by the community," one resident explains, "but at the same time there is a lot of willingness and energy for being there for each other. It just happens naturally." In *The Senior Cohousing Handbook*, Durrett discusses this concern using the example of the fictional "Joe Smith," a previously healthy 60-year-old in a senior cohousing community who has a sudden stroke and wants to return home when he gets out of the hospital. Durrett says that fellow residents would be expected to help provide for some of his daily needs, but exactly which ones would depend on the specific cohousing agreement. "Most likely, the cohousers will take care of a couple of tasks; relatives and friends will do others; insurance will take care of a couple; some will be hired out." However, Durrett emphasizes that this community approach would be an intermediate step to "give Joe's family enough time to find more permanent assistance for him."[5]

The issue of caregiving came home to me after spending time with Henry and Jean Kroll, residents of the Silver Sage Village cohousing development, described earlier. Henry is 68 and Jean is 66, and they've been living at Silver Sage for five years. At age 60, Jean began experiencing memory problems, and this has progressed to the point where she has trouble maintaining focus and completing simple tasks. She has been diagnosed with frontal temporal dementia, and she takes medication and follows a diet and exercise regime in hopes of slowing down the disease. When I met them at Silver Sage, Henry and Jean were just returning from picking up a St. Bernard they were dog-sitting for the next few days. As we strolled through the landscaped courtyard with the dog excitedly sniffing his new environment, Henry explained that cohousing provides a safe, familiar, and caring environment for Jean that gives her great comfort and happiness, and brings him peace of mind. "If I have to go to Denver for a few hours," he says, "I know that Jean is safe here. It's only an acre and she knows her way around the property. She could knock on any of the other 15 doors here and find a friend." Henry can't imagine what their lives would be like if they weren't in cohousing. "We don't have children in town, and, if we were not at Silver Sage Village, I would be spending thousands of dollars for daycare and other support services for Jean, and respite care for myself. Down the road, she may need more care, but we're taking it one day at a time."

One of the challenges of cohousing is the length of time it takes to realize a project that includes site selection, feasibility studies, financing, site planning, construction management, the city approval process, marketing, membership formation, group processes, and facilitation. Silver Sage began with a highly desirable property site rather than potential residents, and it took three years to develop. This was fast in contrast to the 10 years it took Virginia Elder-Spirit Community (www.elderspirit.net) in Abingdon, Virginia. ElderSpirit was founded by a group of people who wanted a retirement community based on a philosophy of late-life spirituality, and it took a decade for them to locate the property, accumulate the resources, and recruit residents. However, it is possible to benefit from the accumulated cohousing knowledge by working with experienced developers and consultants who could streamline some of the process.

Convivium, a seniors cohousing project in Ottawa, has been trying to get off the ground for about four years. Judith Rinfret has been a member for the past two years and has seen membership in the project fall from 18 to its current seven. But, she points out, this is not the first time the group's numbers have declined, only to rise again. One of Convivium's challenges is its desired location—within a half-hour walk of Parliament Hill and close to all amenities. "This type of property is extremely expensive and rare," Judith says, "and even if we were to locate it today, we are in no position at the moment to make an offer. To date, nobody's dared to assess our finances because it's considered too personal. If we don't have the tough discussion about how to finance this project, we'll just continue dabbling." Judith has learned first-hand why cohousing projects take so long to bring to fruition. "The process is so time-consuming," she explains. "It takes a tremendous amount of work and energy and there are so few models, especially when it comes to cohousing for seniors.

So it's easy to lose momentum and people find alternatives. Two of our founding members left because their need for an alternative place to live was urgent and they found a condo. That's been a real loss to the group. Many people who've left the group say, 'Let us know when the project gets off the ground. We're still interested.' I, too, would like someone else to do the work and then move in, but some of us have to make it happen."

In Judith's experience, you need a leader to pull off a project of this magnitude and complexity, and this reality can run up against the cohousing model of decision-making by consensus. "Consensus is great and I agree that many heads are better than one," she says, "but applying it to building, financing, and construction has its drawbacks. The process is slow and it may be difficult or almost impossible to make changes." Despite the challenges, Judith is committed to the project because she wants what cohousing offers. She is 71 and her husband is 73 and they are still living in their large family home with their bedroom on the third floor. "My great-grandmother died at 103, my grandmother died at 100, and my mother is 95 and is still in pretty good shape," she says. "So, I could well have a long life. Watching my family members age, I've learned a lot about what it takes to age well. I realize that good health cannot be taken for granted. And if either of us suddenly had a change in health, we wouldn't be able to stay in our home and we might be forced to accept housing we wouldn't have chosen."

Judith knows they could simply move to a bungalow or a condo but she feels the cohousing concept is worth the effort. "And it's not only the physical support and shared skills," she explains. "We would benefit from the social and psychological dynamics of cohousing. As we get older we become more isolated and less needed. I want to live with people where our opinions and ideas still matter, where I think I can make a difference. It would be lovely to share stories and help one another. It's exciting and stimulating to relate to the various personalities in a group, and we would be more lively by making that effort." To try to succeed, Convivium is refocusing its objectives and has expanded membership to adults of any age, and may even expand further to include families. Judith recognizes that one obvious option is to buy into a pre-existing cohousing complex and avoid the struggles of pulling a project like this up by its bootstraps, but there's nothing currently available where she wants to live. And that's the only non-negotiable for Judith—the location. She wants to live near the action and amenities of downtown Ottawa. "My husband and I are still committed to trying to make it happen," she concludes, "but I really hope it gets off the ground before we're too old to enjoy it."

But cohousing is not for everyone. When Debbie was in her thirties and the single mother of two teenagers she was part of a group that was trying to put together a cohousing project. The members met over a number of years but weren't able to locate a suitable property and the group petered out. Now 66 and living alone, she decided to reinvestigate the concept and went with her sister to look at a cohousing project that she describes as "having everything."

"It was beautifully designed," she describes, "with an organic farm and horses, its own woods, and lovely landscaping. It was at the edge of a vibrant small town so it wasn't isolated. There were mixed age groups with both young families and old people. It was all perfectly lovely," she concludes, "but when we left we both said, 'Spare us.'" She struggles to explain why it didn't appeal to them. "It's hard to know exactly what was wrong with it, but something didn't sit right. It was too perfect, too planned. I need something with a little more grit, more of the fullness of life and room for the unexpected. I have no appetite for conflict or confrontation, but I do need surprise. I felt that I would just go to sleep there. I need to find ways to be stimulated without being agitated."

Her visit made Debbie realize that she had lost some of her appetite for participatory living. "I have very little tolerance now for working committees. I don't want to have to form a new community and figure out the rules and decide things like what to do if somebody leaves. I want to get together with people but I don't want the functioning of the community to be the focus. I'm losing my patience for these kinds of demands. So I need to find a community where these expectations are minimal. Yet I am both nourished by the community and can nourish others. So I'm looking for a place that will provide me with an engaging social life with less effort." She concludes with a wry smile, "Staying all alone in my own space is not my goal, so I'm willing to give up a bit of my privacy to get this, but there's a limit as to how much."

If you are debating whether cohousing is for you, Diana Leafe Christian's book *Finding Community: How to Join an Ecovillage or Intentional Community* offers guidance. Leafe Christian has been editor of *Communities* magazine since 1993, and her book explores the reasons to join a community, as well as the most common fears. Sections are devoted to visiting and evaluating communities, and the steps to both joining and, if necessary, leaving a community, including sample community membership documents. The book includes information about specific communities from a range of types including elder cohousing, senior housing co-ops, homesteading communities, spiritual and Christian communities, as well as income-sharing communities where people pool their incomes and share a common treasury. A chapter is devoted to what it takes to live in a community and includes a description of those who do well in community living and those who don't, although this section does betray her pro-community bias. For example, she says that someone who would do well in a community has a healthy sense of self, is willing to abide by group agreement, and is willing to find a balance between community goals and personal goals. On the other hand, people who don't do well in a community are those who are angry and impatient much of the time, or those used to getting their own way, being the boss, or having their orders followed without question. Useful advice includes how to evaluate a community in terms of your own needs and vision, and the book would be helpful as well in evaluating the forms of intentional community discussed in the upcoming section on Religious/Ethnocultural/Spiritual Communities.

Those involved in the design or redesign of an intentional community could benefit from Peter Block's book, *Community: The Structure of Belonging*, which includes a chapter on how to design physical space in order to support community. Block emphasizes the importance of the following elements: reception areas that tell us we are in the right place and are welcome; hallways wide enough for intimate seating and casual contact; eating spaces that refresh us and encourage relatedness; meeting rooms designed with nature, art, conviviality, and citizen-to-citizen interaction in mind; and large community spaces that have the qualities of communal intimacy.[6]

Seniors Housing

ANOTHER STRATEGY for housing ourselves is to work with organizations to expand options for senior home ownership. Often, such projects are undertaken by organizations with a religious, spiritual, or cultural focus, as discussed in the next section, but in this section we look at examples where the sponsors are social service clubs or purpose-built organizations. In the section Reasons for Optimism, you were introduced to the Mature Action Committee (MAC) of Whistler, British Columbia, the non-profit organization incorporated in 1995 for the purpose of advocating for seniors housing. Whistler is a small resort municipality with a youthful population—only 5 per cent of the population is over 65—so making the case for seniors housing hasn't been easy. As Sue Lawther, president of MAC, explains, "Whistler does not see itself as a place housing people with walkers. But we have many more seniors who are permanent residents than people imagine, and many of us have no intention of moving away." In the early to mid-nineties, some community members started to realize that seniors were being forced to leave Whistler because they lacked housing options. "There were some smaller condos available," Sue says, "but they were not affordable. So unless you had a million dollars, there was no opportunity to downsize. It was quite difficult to get support for this issue because people assumed that seniors who lived here were well off and could take care of themselves. We weren't looking for a subsidy; it was simply the case that the marketplace wasn't going to respond to our needs. Whistler had a cap on development and we're very close to build-out, so it didn't make economic sense for developers to build for seniors. So we needed a new approach. Our goal is not just to target lower income seniors, we want to expand the choices for everyone. And our intent is not to provide seniors housing that outsiders will flock to, but rather to look after Whistler's own as they age."

Gord Leidal, past president of MAC, describes the years of step-by-step effort that is starting to see results. "In 2001, we raised money among ourselves to hire a planning consultant," he explains. "We did a needs survey to assess people's interests: did they prefer to rent or own, what could they afford, and what sort of housing were they looking for." Then MAC looked for potential building sites that could be developed for seniors housing. They focused on crown land because they couldn't afford to buy on the market. "Armed with this information we went to the municipality," Gord says. "They agreed to set up a Seniors Housing Task Force, and we came back with a set of recommendations, which they adopted. MAC was not asking for subsidization, but we knew some stimulus was required and we requested amnesty zoning for locations with potential for senior housing. Of the three areas identified by council, one development is built and occupied, lots have been zoned in another project, and the third is on hold."

The project that is up and running is Cheakamus Crossing, which was part of the athletes' village for the 2010 Olympics. The development consists of 24 condos—six townhomes and 18 apartments. When the development went on the market, the townhomes were oversubscribed three to one, but only a handful of the apartments were purchased. "Part of the challenge is that the condo apartments were not designed from the seniors' point of view," Gord explains. "The parking is not accessible to the building and used to be open, although it has since been covered. Also, there was a two-year waiting period from the time of placing your deposit to move-in. It's tough for seniors to put up money under those conditions, especially if it's not an ideal fit. And by the time the project was up and running, some of the early MAC participants who wanted to move into seniors housing had either passed away or had been forced to move away. So, when seniors were not prepared to buy in, the condos were offered more broadly to buyers. However, when the units come back on the market, they will always be offered first to seniors."

Sue Lawther was able to buy one of the townhomes in Cheakamus Crossing and predicts the apartments will become more and more desirable over time. "The percentage of people who are over 75 is going to increase in Whistler," she says, "and they'll want the elevator in the lobby. And these apartments are more affordable. For now, my husband and I are happy in the townhome because we want the front-door ground-level entry with a garage, and we need the extra space because we still have grandchildren visiting. But downsizing to an apartment will be our next step."

Gord cautions that developing seniors housing has its challenges, including the length of time required to bring the projects to market, coupled with seniors' self-perceptions. "In a small community like ours it's a really big challenge to get 20 to 25 seniors to all agree to move together, two years in advance," he says. "And then we have to ask people to put down a deposit on a deal that's not going to be completed for over two years. This is particularly difficult when the market is risky and the real estate market is somewhat depressed. There's also a problem with people's self-perception. They don't think they're old, so why would they need seniors housing? We did a survey in 2009 asking people to rate their overall health and many of them rated their health as excellent. But these same people were receiving a long list of medical services including dialysis and treatments for conditions like hypertension and diabetes. So we've had to relax the age-restricted requirements somewhat. We accept that *mature adults* aren't necessarily seniors, but we need to fill up the units. And the units will keep on turning over, with priority for resale going to seniors. We considered cohousing as another approach to developing seniors housing but concluded it was no more attractive in terms of affordability than what we're doing. In fact, once you factor in all the common areas, it's less affordable."

If your organization decides to tackle senior housing, Gord emphasizes the importance of establishing collaborative networks. "Partnering with the Whistler Housing Authority has been very important. And nothing would have happened without the amnesty zoning, and for that we needed the political will. To get that you have to educate people." Sue agrees and says, "It's all about the data. Do your homework and let the facts speak for themselves. We need to recognize that if we give seniors better housing options and a supportive community, they will be more self-supporting. And not only self-supporting, we're prepared to help one another, and we have a lot to offer to our community as a whole. What we're working on is a paradigm shift in our way of thinking about aging in place in our community."

In Winnipeg, it was the Knights of Columbus of St. Vital that undertook development of St. Vital Knights Villa, a non-profit housing project for "seasoned citizens." The 48-unit complex, housing one- and two-bedroom suites in a variety of sizes, is a life lease facility open to people aged 55 and older. A life lease is a legal agreement that permits the purchaser to occupy a dwelling unit for life in exchange for a lump sum payment (entrance fee) and a monthly payment to cover the project management fees and maintenance and operating costs. St. Vital Knights Villa includes a multi-purpose space with kitchenette facilities, games room, lounge, meeting/library, hair care, workshop, common storage space, and exercise room. The Knights have the philosophy that a "home" is more than a "shelter" and have provided this communal space for recreational and social activities with the goal of promoting a harmonious community. The Villa's landscaped grounds include an area designated for garden plots and the city of Winnipeg plans to develop a park on the riverbank lands between the Villa and the adjacent Seine River.[1] In 2011, the senior residents launched a gardening project with youngsters at a neighbouring daycare. They allocated a garden plot and together planted beans, peas, tomatoes, and onions. At harvest time, the seniors held a barbecue for the children and daycare staff. The director of the daycare says the connection between the generations is particularly important to these children because many of them are immigrants or refugees and have no extended family living nearby. "It's like adopted grandparents," she says.[2] The Knights of Columbus have sponsored several life lease projects across Manitoba. The Winnipeg River Manor in the village of Powerview, about 90 minutes north of Winnipeg, might appeal to outdoor enthusiasts given its claim of being close to some of the best walleye fishing in the province.[3]

The first life lease projects in Canada were developed in Manitoba and Saskatchewan in the late 1980s. Most projects are sponsored by community-based non-profit organizations, and the major difference between a life lease and a condominium is that the title to the life lease unit is held by the sponsoring organization, not the resident. Usually the housing is classed as affordable because of the non-profit nature of the operation, and the project sponsor may contain the costs by donating land, capital, and/or labour. There are now several hundred projects in existence, mostly in Manitoba and Ontario, and their legal status and structure vary widely from one province to the next. For example, in Manitoba life lease residents are considered tenants and are subject to the Landlord and Tenant Act, whereas in Saskatchewan and Alberta, life lease residents are viewed neither as owners nor as tenants, but as purchasers of a life interest in their unit, and are required to pay property taxes. In some provinces, the consumer must pay the full entrance fee at move-in while others allow financing. The amount of the monthly fee depends on the size of the initial lump sum. There is also variation in how the upfront financial payment is refunded to the outgoing residents or their estates. In some cases life lease holders get the same amount back that they paid in, in other situations units change hand at market value, while in other cases consumers receive the original fee augmented by a value increase tied to an index such as the Consumer Price Index.[4]

In 2007, CMHC published a report on life lease housing, *An Examination of Life Lease Housing Issues*, that looked at 15 developments in five provinces. When they consulted with focus groups of residents, all the participants said they would buy a life lease unit again and would advise a friend to purchase one. "While some had mild concerns about their units or the financial arrangements, the strong sense of community in these complexes more than offset any of these concerns. Residents indicated that they were extremely happy in their choice of housing." Based on the complexity of this type of investment and the evidence from the focus groups that not everyone understood the nature of what they had purchased, the report concluded that seniors should be encouraged to seek professional advice before purchasing a life lease interest. For example, life lease purchasers need to understand that, compared to condo owners, they have limited control over decisions about management of the building. Also, the normal risks related to the value of the asset at sale are greater due to lack of legislative protection in some jurisdictions, as well as the restriction to sell only to seniors. The report also advised the non-profit sponsors, for whom this may be their first real estate development, to get assistance with the process to avoid financial and reputation problems.[5]

The BC Non-Profit Housing Association report *Financing Seniors' Housing Projects Using Resident Equity* is a good resource if you are considering working with an organization to sponsor a life lease project. The document includes detailed case studies, key success factors, and a summary list of steps to development. The report concluded that life leases have the potential to be successful given the right ingredients in the development stages. One of the critical success factors is the strength of the sponsoring organization. Because life leases are complex and time-consuming to develop, sponsors must be committed and have appropriate expertise. The report concludes that life leases seem to be easier to develop successfully when they are sponsored by groups with strong affiliations, such as churches, ethnic groups, or service clubs. However, other kinds of sponsors can be successful, and the report cited the example of a sponsor that originated in a church but expanded its membership to the broader community among their board members.[6]

Religious/
Ethnocultural/
Spiritual
Communities

AS WE CONSIDER our options for housing ourselves as we age, some of us are turning to religious, ethnocultural, or spiritual communities. Our motivations are multiple and often overlapping. We may appreciate the sense of shared values. We may long to speak the language of our childhood, or celebrate cultural holidays or religious ceremonies. We may appreciate food that is geared to our palate and fellow residents who have a shared sense of history. And the housing may be more affordable. For Gwen, the link to her church is practical as well as emotional. "I'm 70 years old and I'm being very strategic," she says. "I belonged to a church that was closed because there were not enough people in the congregation to keep it viable. So I've started going to a bigger church that runs a seniors home. The home has one-bedroom apartments, rent geared to income, and I think I will meet their criteria by age 77, when I hope to move in."

Nola has been an active member of her church for decades and she played a central role in the church's project to build housing for homeless women. The building houses 42 women, 20 of whom are seniors. The light-filled building was purpose-built with a quiet room, computer lab, and exercise space and a patio area in the back. The seniors eat their meals together in the dining room. More recently, Nola was a member of the Affordable Housing Committee that worked with a local developer to build affordable condos. "The idea was that someone with an annual income of $55,000 or less could buy a unit," she explains, "and the development fees were waived so it was manageable. My brother bought two units for my husband and me to live in when our house became too much. My husband had been severely handicapped because of a stroke and was in a wheelchair. It's a great location and would have been perfect for us, but my husband died. Now that I'm alone, I'm not ready. So I'm renting these units out on my brother's behalf at $700 per month, when a similar unit elsewhere would rent for $1,100 per month. I'm 70 years old now, and, from a long-term point of view, the condo will work perfectly. It's part of a community that has multiple ages and should give me opportunities to participate in all kinds of things. Plus it's a great location where I can walk to everything I need."

In Palo Alto, California, the Jewish community has taken a holistic view of housing their seniors by imbedding the Moldaw Family Residences for seniors in the Taube Koret Campus for Jewish Life. The Campus is a destination for people of all ages and the goal is to ensure that the senior residents are an integral part of the Jewish community. Moldaw comprises eight linked houses containing 193 units on the pedestrian-friendly Campus with art studios, a library and business centre, multiple dining venues, and a spa/salon. The Campus links Moldaw with the Oshman Family Jewish Community Center, which offers teen and adult meeting spaces, a cultural centre, and child daycare. By offering classes with local experts, guest lectures, performances, and discussion groups, the Campus is conceived as a place for students of all ages. By integrating the community, younger people share with seniors, and the Campus has a sense of different generations.[1]

The campus concept is part of the design, as well, at Hesperus Village (www.hesperus.ca) in Thornhill, Ontario, a seniors housing complex located on the campus of the Toronto Waldorf School. Hesperus is surrounded by green space on a wooded ravine along the East Don River. Along with the school, the campus includes the Rudolf Steiner Centre for teacher education, community gardens, and a weekly farmers' market. The Waldorf philosophy is based on anthroposophy, a way of thinking espoused by the Austrian philosopher Rudolf Steiner that encourages a humanistic approach for caring for one another within a community.

Hesperus is very wide-ranging in its philosophical approach and suggests their facilities would be suitable for "people who value community and wish to contribute to communal life; who are drawn to a spiritual and contemplative life; who enjoy natural surroundings and gardening; and who support and enjoy a variety of cultural and artistic endeavours." The first Hesperus building, constructed in 1987, has 77 units, including bachelors and one- and two-bedroom suites, and a 2001 addition has 33 one-bedroom and 27 two-bedroom apartments. The rents are affordable, with half of the units geared to income. Residents may choose to enjoy communal meals and participate in a variety of social, cultural, spiritual, and gardening activities. There is an on-site medical clinic with physicians offering both conventional and holistic care, and personal support workers are available as needed. Sybille Hahn, a resident and Hesperus Village's volunteer coordinator, explained why the Village has so many two-bedrooms when most social housing for seniors is built with bachelors and one-bedrooms. "We thought old age could be a time of sharing an apartment again," she says. "We have mothers and daughters on our waiting list and a couple with a grown son who would sometimes stay with them. Or there could be sisters or a couple of seniors who are friends and would be willing to share. It's like why we wanted the walls not to be perfectly square in all the apartments. Square rooms lead to inside-the-box thinking. At Hesperus, we try to break out of that."[2]

Kendal Communities has been providing non-profit housing for the elderly in the Quaker tradition since 1973 and now operates in eight states in the United States with about 3,300 residents in 11 communities. The basic Quaker principles of equality, peace, simplicity, integrity, and community guide Kendal's work. Their communities vary as to the extent of support services available. For example, in order to gain admittance to what Kendal calls a continuing care retirement community (CCRC), residents usually must be able to care for themselves. Residents of the CCRC are described as typically healthy, active adults who want security about their future health care. The CCRC concept is similar to the life lease described in Seniors Housing, with the resident paying an entrance fee and ongoing monthly fees. But in this case, the resident can receive comprehensive on-site health care for life. Kendal puts an emphasis on the residents organizing the social, cultural, intellectual, and spiritual life of the community and typically doesn't employ activities directors, except in health-centre settings for residents who need assistance. They believe that independence and self-sufficiency are supported, in part, by *not* providing some services that community members are able to provide for themselves. They emphasize that, after joining a Kendal community, many residents continue to be involved in the wider world, remaining active in political, cultural, volunteer, and religious activities, and some continue with full- or part-time work. The Quaker tradition of lifelong learning and community engagement has led to formal links being established with nearby colleges and universities in some of the communities.

Five years ago, 80-year-old Anne Elder moved with her husband to the Kendal community in Oberlin, Ohio, from the Washington, D.C., area so that she could work with Oberlin College and the city on their sustainable development programs. "Moving here, we have a chance to be a crucial part of a sustainable city," she says. "I've always been concerned about environmental and energy issues, so this is important to me."[3] When Marjean Willett was 75 years of age she moved to Kendal at Longwood, a community of 300 residents in Kennett Square, Pennsylvania. Ten years later she reports being "delighted" to be there. "Since then I have had a hip replacement (my second)," she says, "made many new friends, made many trips, and have been continually encouraged to learn new things and take on new responsibilities."[4]

When it comes to assisted living or chronic care facilities, people with strong linguistic, cultural, or religious ties may seek out facilities designed for their community. Being surrounded by the familiar can have significant health benefits, and the sense of community can reduce social isolation and depression. For Margot, it's all about the quality of the caregiving, and she was able to locate superb care for her mother at a nursing home that catered to her mother's Italian language, culture, and food preferences. From Margot's experience, facilities with a religious or cultural focus seem to have the edge in attracting and keeping excellent staff. "What it comes down to is the quality of the person caring for you," she says, "because you're dependent, vulnerable, and at their mercy. My mother's caregivers told me they were her real family, and in many ways that was true. We need to inculcate that attitude into the system, so that being a caregiver is a respected profession that will attract our young people. We need a change in attitude in facilities who think that good geriatric care is about more money for fresh flowers or new upholstery."

The director of care at the Yee Hong Centre for Geriatric Care, with locations in Mississauga and Scarborough, Ontario, agrees that their success is attributable to their staff. The Centre's culture results in high staff retention rates and they support this culture by seeking out best practices from other care facilities. Yee Hong is geared toward serving the Chinese population with services that include Chinese food, Tai Chi, and karaoke Chinese opera. Their data show that their commitment to ethnocultural care has resulted in reduced weight loss, lower rates of depression, and fewer falls, skin ulcers, and hospitalization among the centre's residents as compared with those in mainstream homes.[5]

Even if we don't belong to a specific religious, ethnocultural, or spiritual community, or wouldn't share completely its philosophy or taste in food, we shouldn't rule out a conversion. This may sound a bit tongue-in-cheek, but as you can see from these examples, there is much to be gained from participating in a community that values older people and is paying attention to our quality of life. In *Remind Me Who I Am, Again*, author Linda Grant writes about trying to find a facility for her mother in England after she had been diagnosed with dementia. She quotes a social worker who always asks her clients if they are Jewish "because a Jewish home was the very best kind." "'Are you sure you're not Jewish?' she would enquire urgently. 'Think. Think.

Even a Jewish grandmother. I know you're black and from Jamaica but are you absolutely sure . . . ?'"[6] If you decide to go the route of engaging with the community of your choice, you'll need to start now to participate actively. Last-minute conversions will have little chance of success. These facilities are oversubscribed for the very reasons we think they're desirable. For example, the wait time to get into the Yee Hong Centre for Geriatric Care can be a decade.[7] As for Hesperus Village, units open up infrequently, and in January 2012, there was a waiting list of about 120 people.[8] So if you want to age with your chosen community, the best option would be to work with them now to develop new seniors housing options that might be there when you need them.

Supportive Housing

SUPPORTIVE HOUSING provides the kind of assistance we talked about in the Community Support section, but under our own roof. If the financial resources are available, we could engage our own caregiver and modify our home to include space for their accommodation. If our own needs were sufficiently limited, we could share our caregiver with a number of neighbours. For the parents of my friend Nancy, this process happened informally. They live in downtown Montreal in an apartment building where the seniors are aging in place. The concierge has connected the caregivers who are already working part-time in the building with other tenants who require assistance.

Another option would be to live collectively in a supportive facility. When news came out recently about the launch of the Baba Yagas seniors housing project for aging feminists in Montreuil, a suburb of Paris, many women sent me the details, saying this project was their ideal. The 25-apartment building with below-market rents will be managed as a collective, and the tenants—women aged 60 to 90—will take care of each other. The group decided to call themselves the "Baba Yagas," a term in Slavic folklore for old witches. An apartment will be reserved for a nurse or health aide and four apartments will be reserved for young people. Presumably the youth will be available to do some chores, including heavy lifting, in exchange for reduced rent. Eighty-four-year-old Therese Clerc waged a 10-year battle for the public funds to build the project because she didn't want to live alone. She was afraid it would be dangerous and the solitude would be crushing. She rejected, as well, the model of the old folks home. "We don't want to be old ladies all sitting in front of a television," she says. "I'm a night-bird and late riser, so dinners at 6 p.m.—no thanks!" Instead, she wanted to "age joyously" with other women and "remain intelligent and active." Various levels of government in France have expressed an interest in the Baba Yagas model, assuming it would cost less than paying to keep elderly people at home or in retirement homes, and similar initiatives are under way in Brest, Lyon, and other French cities. The project appears to have gained support because of the death of the elderly during the heat wave in the summer of 2003, which forced France to re-examine its senior policies.[1]

Abbeyfield provides seniors with another version of supportive housing by offering them a home of their own in their local community in a small household comprising seven to 10 seniors. The non-profit organization, founded in 1956 in the UK to provide supportive housing, currently operates 800 houses in 17 countries. In 1984, Abbeyfield Canada was established and now has 40 societies and 28 houses under its auspices, with ten more planned or under construction. A typical Abbeyfield House provides a bed-sitting room and private bathroom for each resident, who is free to furnish and decorate the rooms as they choose. Common areas are shared. A live-in house coordinator provides two home-cooked meals a day, eaten in a communal dining room. Breakfast is usually a self-serve buffet. Most houses also include a garden or outdoor area. The house coordinator has a self-contained suite and manages the building, while also coordinating volunteers who offer day-to-day support for duties such as garden maintenance. Residents pay their share of the running costs, including food. Because Abbeyfield is not a nursing home, residents should not need any long-term nursing care.

Each Abbeyfield House is administered by a non-profit society, sometimes in association with a church or service club. Local societies run individual houses with autonomy in matters of day-to-day operations and operate under the guidance of the national organization, according to certain guiding principles. The national office, located in Toronto, is administered by a volunteer board of directors. Their website (www.abbeyfield.ca) provides instructions about how to form a society and offers guidance on governance, building management, fundraising, events management, promotional strategies, and resident recruitment.

Kingsley has watched the development of a number of Abbeyfield homes. He finds that one of the challenges with operating a small facility is to find compatible residents who get along with one another. "You have to get the right people as residents," he explains, "because when you're living in such close proximity to so few people there aren't many buffers. If there are lots of applicants, then you can screen people to get the right fit. But, if your house isn't in a financial position to say 'no' to paying customers, then you're stuck with people we might not want as our daily dinner companions. Having said this, many houses have a wonderful, vibrant group of residents who really enjoy one another's company."

The Saanich Peninsula Abbeyfield Housing Society is expanding upon the concept of supportive housing in small households with their plan for a Campus of Care on 34 acres of land in Saanich, British Columbia. The Society is raising the funds to purchase the land from Saanich Peninsula communities through donations and loans. The long-term strategy is to build a facility that will provide a spectrum of housing and care for seniors, to allow them to age in place and end the separation of elderly couples in the last years of their lives.[2]

Another way that seniors find supportive housing is by living in a private residence that is operated as a small group home. The home is usually owned and operated by a family or an individual interested in supplementing their income. As an example, the Seniors Community Programs of the Niagara Region in Ontario offers supportive housing in residences in Fort Erie, Port Colborne, and Welland, in private or semi-private accommodations in both rural and urban settings. The resident's fee is based on income and the residences are selected, inspected, and approved by municipal, regional, and provincial authorities. The degree of help provided is in keeping with resident abilities and could include meals and snacks, personal care, linen and laundry services, housekeeping, medication prompts, monitoring, and referral to community resources, recreation, social and spiritual activities, and participation in community outings. This is a housing option for people who are independent, and physically and mentally able to care for themselves; individual care needs are assessed before a residence is selected.[3]

Other organizations provide supportive housing by partnering with a senior service provider. The OWN Housing Co-op, the 142-unit building in Toronto described earlier, partners with Dixon Hall, a non-profit social service agency, to provide its residents with in-house personal support/care services. Ninety-year-old Ethel Meade, a co-op resident for 11 years, explained in an interview how the service works. She describes waking up and being unable to put weight on her knee and contacting Dixon Hall's Supportive Housing Program. "I phoned them, they arrived in half an hour with a wheelchair, they took me to a clinic, took me to a hospital for an X-ray, and loaned me a walker." She says, "The main point is peace of mind—to know that if you need help, you'll get it."[4] Dixon Hall provides its services to seniors in three non-profit buildings located not far from one another.[5]

In North York, Ontario, Circle of Care launched a pilot project to provide "cluster care" to four apartment buildings with a large senior population. Services include individual and group interventions, personal support, meal delivery, transportation, adult day programs, and social work services. The non-profit organization, which began in 1974 by coordinating services for Jewish elderly in Toronto, has now expanded to serve people of many faiths and cultures and all ages. More than 7,000 people a year receive services from 525 staff members and 320 volunteers with the goal of helping people live healthier, happier, and longer lives in their homes.[6] In another cluster care pilot project carried out by the South Fraser Health Region of British Columbia, the majority of the people served were women over the age of 80. A report on the successful outcomes of the project includes detailed recommendations for replicating the program elsewhere.[7]

An interesting variation on the supportive building is the supportive cul de sac, an innovative solution to community support that Lorna and her neighbours are trying to put in place. Six families who live in the same cul de sac are talking about jointly purchasing a house in their neighbourhood to house a caregiver. Of the 10 people who are involved at this stage, three are over 80, a couple are in their seventies, and the rest are 65. "We might be able to get a total of 15 people who would jointly purchase a property," Lorna explains. "Ideally, we would find a family to live there and support us where both the husband and wife are personal support workers. Only people who have bought into the property and sponsored the family would have access to their services. I can also see us helping each other, doing things like compiling grocery lists for shopping, for example." Lorna says that the plan would require people to modify their own homes for the long term. "Two of the families have a master bedroom on the ground floor," she says, "and the others would be prepared to put in a lift to access the master on the second floor." The neighbours are motivated to try and make this work.

"We're all concerned about the cost of living," Lorna explains. "If we follow this model, it would be a lot cheaper to stay where we are, and the property we purchase might even prove to be a good investment. Many of us would love to stay right here. We have a mixed community of all ages where kids play hockey on the street. Our families are of different ages, we appreciate different cultures, most of us are dog lovers, we participate in the birth of grandchildren and celebrations. We notice when things aren't going well for people and try to help. It's a real community. We could downsize to a condo but that wouldn't necessarily improve our quality of life. Condo life doesn't necessarily bring people together, and we could end up being more isolated and alone. But we know we won't be able to stay here without support. Hopefully, we'll get some support from government services, but we won't be able to count on them for everything. You can't even count on them now and things are only going to get worse. Our next step is to canvas the broader group on our cul de sac about this idea and figure how much support there is. Our group's unanimous sentiment is, 'We would never become a burden on our children.'"

Continuum of Care

WHILE all the above housing options are supportive, they don't provide the continuum of care that would be needed if our care needs were to increase. Some people who move to a retirement home are trying to make it their last move. If this is their goal, they'll need a facility with the capacity to support their increasing care needs, even should they become critical. Margot is in her sixties and has given a good deal of thought to how she can maintain her quality of life as she ages. "My health issues make me older than my chronological age," she explains, "so my preference would be to live in a graduated care community. Since I already have some physical limitations, I know I'm not going to be well and I don't want to have to adjust. So I would like to be able to continue living in the same place but move to different parts of the community as I become increasingly dependent. As for my family, they need their own lives. I don't want them to have to take on the care and feeding of their parents."

What Margot is looking for is labelled the "continuum of care." In his book *The Geography of Aging: Preparing Communities for the Surge in Seniors*, community and regional planner Gerald Hodge recommends that we plan for "Senior-Smart" communities using the tenet of *continuum of care*, along with *seniors' independence*.[1] The *continuum of care* recognizes five stages of senior wellness, each covering a distinct domain of care with its own standards and professional training. The continuum moves from well elderly, to the frail elderly living at home, to the functionally impaired elderly living at home, to the functionally impaired elderly living in facilities requiring round-the-clock medical care, to the ill elderly who require intensive medical care. The "Senior-Smart" community would support us to move seamlessly from one stage to the next.[2]

Debbie's parents lived in a facility with this arrangement and she remembers thinking it was ideal. "My parents downsized from their big house when they were 70 and moved to an adult community," she recalls. "But when they turned 80, my mother said if anything happens to either of us, the other one shouldn't be left to pick up the pieces. So they moved to a seniors community on a 70-acre property that had been set up by retired professors. The organizers had put their intellectual stamp on the facility and included a huge library and stimulating programming. There were woods, a tennis court, and amazing programs. Everyone lived in independent apartments, but there was also an assisted-living facility. The plan was that you never had to leave. My parents lived there until they were 93 years of age. During this period, my father developed dementia and my mother had access to all kinds of support for him. By the end of their lives we were paying for extra help with round-the-clock care, but it was all available for a price. Fortunately their money lasted, because they had planned only on living to 85. I felt that I could live in this place. If you still had your physical mobility, you could be out playing tennis, and if you'd kept your mental ability, you could be constantly stimulated. And you got to stay there, in what had become your home, right to the end."

Luther Village on the Park in Waterloo, Ontario, was built on this philosophy of "aging-in-place" and offers a range of services and care choices that can be adjusted according to the residents' changing needs. The facility is operated by Lutherwood, a not-for-profit community service agency of the Lutheran Church. The complex, designed for people over 55, includes life lease suites and townhomes, as well as assisted living rental suites. There are 72 townhomes, plus 153 units in the main building, spread over 20 acres. As of July 2012, there were 300 life lease residents and 146 assisted living residents. The five-floor assisted-living centre offers three options: units with full kitchen for those who require minimal support and one meal per day provided, full-service suites including three meals per day, and enhanced care suites in a secure wing with around-the-clock support staff. The Village is forming a partnership with Wilfred Laurier University to provide residents with education programs, and because of the facility's proximity to the university there are ex-professors and academics among the residents. The facility includes a wellness centre, business centre, hair salon, multi-denominational chapel, art gallery, and restaurant, and there are dozens of clubs that focus on activities such as pottery, card games, computers, yoga, and gardening. The Waterloo Recreation Complex is right next door. A volunteer board of directors oversees the operations of the Village with input from a resident advisory board.

The Luther Village website (www.luthervillage.org) includes a video of interviews with residents, including Andrew and Margaret Brockett. Andrew says, "We chose Luther Village because it gives us an opportunity to age in one place, and to stay somewhere where we will build up a community before we get too old. And we also chose it because it's such a beautiful place, and because of its location." Luther on the Village says, "Residents will never again have to cut the grass, shovel the snow, do landscaping, do minor maintenance, or worry about who to call in an emergency."

Retirement Residences

THE MARKETPLACE is responding to the demands of healthy oldsters with retirement residences that are more like boutique hotels than nursing homes. By saving their money and delaying move-in until very late in life, some seniors are able to benefit from facilities that cater to mind, body, and soul with everything from classrooms to yoga rooms, and gyms to gourmet restaurants. Virginia's residence has over 200 residents and she appreciates both the variety of people and the services that come with the size. The residence has a private recital hall/movie theatre with comfortable, banked seating; a private trainer for the fitness room, and a full-time activities coordinator focused on creating stimulating daily programming. In the winter she can swim in the pool, sit in the gazebo in the glass-domed English Garden room surrounded by lush foliage, or have a therapeutic mini-vacation in the tropical room complete with sand, sun simulator, and palm trees.

After Peter's wife died he sold their bungalow and moved into a high-end retirement residence. That was a year ago, and he's now 90 years old and very happy with his decision. "The staff is absolutely fabulous," he says. "They're very friendly, very helpful, and everybody knows your name. My apartment has a full-sized kitchen so I don't need to eat all my meals in the dining room but their food is superb. I invite lots of friends for lunch and dinner, and I've reserved the annex to the dining room for private gatherings." Peter figures his money will last as long as he does, but if he needs more care, the costs will increase. "I could live for another ten years," Peter estimates. "I use the exercise facility three times a week and I'm getting much better core strength. My savings will last—even if I need to buy more services. I could get them to remind me to take my medicine, help me in and out of bed, and provide meals in my apartment, but everything will cost."

Mealtimes are a highlight of the day for many people in retirement residences, and one feature that distinguishes the newer facilities is the presence of a hostess who seats people when they arrive. This creates a different atmosphere from the more traditional approach of being assigned a table and having the same tablemates for lunch and dinner. "Here the hostess seats you with different people every time, so you get to move around," Peter explains. "The hostess knows everyone and will say 'I'm putting you with so and so. You'll enjoy them.' Friends of mine are in another facility and they're really unhappy because they've been assigned a permanent table with people who don't open their mouths. My friends have tried showing up at the tail end of the lunch period, hoping the other people will have left the table already, but so far it's not working."

The quality of the staff is a huge component of resident satisfaction. "The staff really does a bang-up job," Peter says. "They host a breakfast for the ladies and one for the men. Once a week they have a cocktail social with a music combo that plays for an hour. They serve canapés and the whole staff participates. It gives you a homey atmosphere."

Most residences offer trial stays, and taking advantage of this option is recommended. But no matter how good the residence, the adjustment will take time. "I was told to allow myself at least three months before I would feel at home," Peter says. "But it took longer than three months. If you're lucky you'll find a handful of people who can become your friends. I think many people find it difficult to be here because they've moved from familiar surroundings and all of a sudden they don't know anyone. Many of us are here because we're widows or widowers and we need some help. It takes people a while to loosen up. One woman is already moving out and she's barely been here three months. She probably didn't do her homework. Sometimes people move a bit too quickly."

Betsy did considerable planning to get into the retirement residence of her choice, and made some astute financial moves to afford the fees. When she was 75 she moved out of her rental apartment and bought a condo. At the same time, she put her name on a waiting list to move into a retirement residence at age 82. "It was a good thing I bought the condo and stopped renting," she explains. "I was able to put the rental money into the mortgage and now I only have a small mortgage left. The condo has probably doubled in value, judging from the sale of my neighbour's condo, which sold in two days for more than she asked. But even with my increased nest egg, if I live to be 100, I'll run out of money. I'll probably have enough until age 95. But one of the reasons I chose this particular residence is that it's a charitable non-profit organization and, if I run out of funds, I'm pretty sure they won't kick me out." Although Betsy has had a number of health challenges, she's managing very well in her condo and has developed a community of friends. "I have nice neighbours and am part of a book club," she explains, "but I figure it's better to go to the residence sooner rather than later. I'm going to have a small apartment in the independent living section and they'll cook me lunch and dinner. I am tired of cooking for myself. Cooking for one is not very interesting, and I don't like to eat alone in restaurants. Also, it will be nice to have someone drive me here and there. And I can go on their outings and around to events."

Marilou moved into her high-end retirement residence when she was 82 and has no regrets. "At first I felt embarrassed," she said. "I thought it was quite a bit over the top. But I'd looked at other facilities and found far more people at the 'walker stage.' People are much fitter here. I rejected another residence because there was no kitchen, and I wanted to be able to cook. Here I have a fully equipped kitchen with a full-sized fridge. I have a one-bedroom with a small study and a balcony, and my computer is set up in a small extra room. I chose this apartment because its view of the trees reminded me of my childhood and camping. I needed the walk-in shower because I haven't been able to use a bathtub for the past four years. I like to do a lot of entertaining and I have friends here for lunch in the dining room and the food is really good." The only thing that worries Marilou is the possibility that she might outlive her resources. "I have had some wakeful nights," she says. "I sold my home before I moved in and am using that money. Before I made the decision I took my time and consulted with two financial advisors. I have no obligations and no debts. They crunched the numbers and I sold my house at the anticipated price so I achieved the bottom line. I assumed an annual 2 per cent increase in rent. For budgeting purposes I assumed I'd live to 95. My father was 91 when he died and my mother was 86. But it's my cousin who really worries me. At one point she said she'd hate to reach 104, and she lived to be nearly 108." Marilou has chronic sciatica and when it's at it's worst she is immobilized. If she needs more assistance with daily living, things will get more complicated, but she is philosophical. "When and if I need a lot of help I'll be in trouble," Marilou says, "because you pay extra for everything, and I won't be able to afford that. I'm just going to live 'posh' as long as possible, and then they'll have to transfer me to the nearby long-term care facility." Marilou's monthly rent is about $5,000, which includes a meal credit that she often exceeds. If her medical needs increase and she is admitted to a government-subsidized long-term care facility, the monthly rental would be less than half her current monthly rent, and it would cover the provision of all meals and care. But she'd be swapping her lovely apartment in hotel-like surroundings for an institutional setting and a lot of those walkers she was trying to avoid.

Lessons Learned

Chronological Age Is a Poor Fortune Teller

As you read through the stories in the book, you would have difficulty linking a person's age with a life stage or a housing need. That's because chronological age is a poor predictor for the outcomes and needs of seniors, and we shouldn't rely on it for our planning. One man of over 100 years of age will be in his own home with minimal support, while a 66-year-old man is in the assisted care section of a retirement residence. We all age differently, and the extent to which we will need supportive environments will vary according to many factors, including our medical history and our genetic makeup. Another critical factor, as we've discussed, will be the extent to which our home is designed to reduce our chance of injury, and whether it is suitable for rehabilitation after a hospital stay. If it is not, we may find, as my parents did, that our home is a thing of the past.

The following stories of Virginia and Ian provide compelling evidence that one's chronological age is a poor fortune teller. Separated in age by over two decades, they moved into the same retirement home in the same year and travelled very different roads to reach their destination. Ian was 66 when he arrived after having suffered a catastrophic stroke the year before that nearly killed him. Ian's ability to live in the assisted living section of this elegant retirement facility was the successful outcome of months of recovery as he gradually moved from hospital to rehabilitation facility, to assisted living home. His therapy included twice-weekly speech classes. Although he has recovered many other faculties, he is unlikely to see any further improvement with his speech. Ian's move into the retirement home, as well as being a testament to his powers of recovery, is a credit to his pre-planning and foresight. He had always lived alone and had delegated powers of attorney for finance and health care to two trusted advisors who sprang into action when he fell ill. His care team also included a family representative, his former secretary, and several friends, and together they were able to wrap up his business, sell his house, and supervise and coordinate his medical care and eventual move to the residence of his choice.

Virginia moved into the same retirement home at age 89 and, as with Ian, this step is a credit to her pre-planning and foresight. Her husband died decades ago and she remained in their condo after his death. By staying in her home as long as possible she was able to conserve her capital and save for an eventual move into a retirement residence. She was planning for a long life and didn't want the high monthly fees of the residence (around $6,300 per month) to outstrip her savings. But she was determined to be in a residence by age 89 or 90. "I wanted to be physically well and mentally bright when I made the move," she explains. "This way I'd still be able to make friends. I also knew I needed to be in good physical and mental condition to be accepted into the type of independent living home I wanted. Since I wasn't in a medical crisis, I was able to take my time. I made the rounds with my daughters to look at my options and discussed the pros and cons with them. After I decided on this residence, I stayed here as a guest for a month, just to check it out. When my temporary stay was successful, I took my time to sell my condo and get the price I needed. By not being in a rush, I was able to wait and get the apartment of my choice—one with two bedrooms, two balconies, and a great view. I moved in a year after my guest stay."

If We Wait Until Something Happens, It Will Be Too Late

Many of us don't intend to do anything about planning for our old age until we get old. And since, as we've already acknowledged, moving is tough, there's a huge incentive for us to sit tight and wait for something to force our hand. When my parents cancelled the moving van that was supposed to take them to a highly desirable retirement residence, they were eliminating their last chance to choose their own future. After they had made their decision, we sat around as a family and I asked them what they were going to do. They told us they had decided to "wait for an accident." That accident arrived a short four months later when my mother fell out of bed and fractured her collarbone. She was taken to the emergency ward and never returned home. After a few weeks in hospital, she was sent to the one long-term care home that had an available bed. It turned out to be a most depressing and unsatisfactory facility, and our family goal became to get her relocated immediately. This proved more challenging than we imagined because, from the system's point of view, she was "satisfactorily housed." Her condition was deteriorating rapidly in response to her grim surroundings, which further limited her options. For the next few months my father took lengthy bus trips to visit her daily, and he very quickly became unable to cope on his own in their home. He moved to a retirement residence that was close to my mother's facility and the house was sold.

My mother's changing care needs and our efforts to get her into acceptable living conditions ended up placing her in six different locations, counting her stays in hospitals, retirement homes, and long-term care facilities. My father followed her around to stay close, sometimes living with her in the same facility, and sometimes in another location within walking distance. Finally, nearly two years after the "accident," we got them together in an excellent long-term care facility that supports their needs. To get the two of them where they are now has drawn on all our family resources and coordinated efforts, and caused my parents a great deal of emotional and physical pain. The most hard-hitting lesson from my parents' experience is that by waiting for their accident, they gave up any chance of controlling their future. Before my mother had her injury, they had many options for highly desirable accommodation, but my mother refused to leave her home because she did not want any more moves. And here is the terrible irony: by choosing inaction, she had to endure six moves in two years, moves that were so traumatizing they dramatically accelerated a downward physical and mental spiral.

When Kathy and her husband, Martin, sold their home of 25 years to downsize to a condo, people thought it was too soon. They were relatively young—Kathy was 65 and her husband was 10 years older—and they were healthy. But, seven years earlier, Martin had fallen down the stairs carrying out the garbage and ruptured his quadriceps tendon. "At this point, we realized our house was not going to be age-friendly," Kathy says. "And I began to hate the stairs. Also, I started to resent the fact that the care and maintenance of the house was taking up more and more of my time. As well, there were the financial considerations. Our house was our nest egg. We don't have pensions and the difference between the sale of the house and the cost of the condo gave us some financial security."

The timing proved to be a godsend. Four years after they moved into the condo, Martin had a stroke. "I'm so grateful we moved when we did," Kathy says. "Although Martin has made remarkable progress since the stroke, his speech has not fully recovered, and he would not have been able to dispose of his possessions in the same way. The whole downsizing process involved a huge amount of selection and distribution and he did it all himself. He donated 19 boxes of his papers to the university and his daughters sat with him as he went through the previous 25 years of his life. Every paper had an anecdote and I could see the joy they had in sharing his accomplishments. He also dealt with three different book dealers. Post-stroke he wouldn't have been able to be so involved, which would have been a catalyst for a great deal of distress."

As well, when Martin came home from the hospital, Kathy was happy to be in a much more manageable environment. "If we had been living in the house, it would have been much harder," Kathy explains. "Because of the stairs, he would have needed someone to be with him at all times. I would have been more nervous, and getting around generally would have been much more work. Here, we go into the parking garage and up the elevator. Martin was completely comfortable in the condo having been here already four years, instead of having to get used to a new environment after the stroke. And we avoided the guilt. Martin would have felt terrible if everything had all fallen on me and I had to do the move alone."

It was the example of her mother that convinced Kathy to plan ahead. "At the time we were considering downsizing, I had just moved my mother into a condo," Kathy explains. "And it was way too late. She should have done it five years earlier. She was used to the suburbs where you have to drive everywhere and she didn't know how to take advantage of the freedom. She was unable to get the pleasure out of living downtown. She said, 'If only I had done this earlier,' and I thought, 'I don't want those words to ever come out of my mouth.' Our huge advantage is that Martin and I were completely in synch on this decision, and that doesn't always happen with couples. We are people who believe in controlling our lives, that's what we teach our children. Why would we release all control at the end of our life?"

Kathy's emphasis on the importance of personal control when making housing decisions later in life is supported by the research findings. ENABLE-AGE, the longitudinal study referred to earlier that looked at the relationship between our home environment and healthy aging, found that seniors who had an internal locus of control had a better sense of well-being. Researchers defined seniors as having an internal locus of control if they thought that they themselves, rather than external influences, were responsible for their housing situation.[1]

Don't Count on This Being Our Last Move

Unless you're moving into a continuum of care facility, the move you're making now may not be your last. So you need to leave yourself room to manoeuvre. Liz assumed she was making a final relocation, twice. Both times she's been wrong. She is 64 years of age and she and her partner moved two times in the last decade searching for the right location to put down final roots. Liz is the one you read about earlier who moved from their 16-acre rural property fearing it might kill them, or their guests. They had bought the beautiful acreage eight years earlier thinking it would be a good place to retire, and they fully intended it to be their last move. Then, when they relocated to a small town, they restored a lovely heritage home and created a beautiful garden, and they assumed once again that this would be their final resting place. But then Liz's son and his wife gave her a grandchild. And now she's longing to live closer to him. But she's worried she won't be able to recoup her investment in their current home. "We bought this beautiful property as our retirement home," she explains, "so we started renovating and agreed we'd keep going until we were both satisfied. But we've sunk too much into it and to get our money back will take several years more, at least. And even if we break even, I wonder whether we'll be able to afford something I like as much in another location. And if not, the big question is whether I'd be ready to give up having a nice home and garden." Liz is not sure she could face another move because she knows herself well. "Each time we've relocated we have extensively renovated the new house, and I know I'll want to do that with any new home," she says. "I don't want to move into a place that someone has already redone. I want to find a fabulous place with good potential and do it myself. But then there is the emotional pressure of spending too much money. And there is such physical exhaustion around a move that I can see why people sometimes decide it's easier just to stay put. The physical and emotional battles that take place during a move are stupendous. So we might just stay where we are." Here is Liz's advice for the rest of us. "If you decide to relocate to a new community to build your dream home or remodel that heritage building, try to leave enough room in the budget for an escape plan if things don't work out as you hoped or new opportunities beckon."

This need for an escape plan applies at every stage. You'll recall that Virginia stayed as a guest for a month in the retirement residence of her choice, just to make sure. She didn't put her condo on the market until she was certain that the location was right for her. If you're thinking of moving into a seniors residence, it would be wise to go for a lengthy trial stay and hang on to your home until you're sure you're making the right decision. When Gordon was 101, he thought it might be time to move from his apartment to a retirement residence—mainly because he was tired of preparing his own meals. And he thought he would welcome a bit more care and attention. But he hedged his bets by extending his apartment lease and paying for the two locations for a few months, just in case the residence didn't live up to his expectations. His fears were realized. "I felt I gave it a real try," Gordon said. "I got a great room in the residence and bought terrific-looking furniture and had everything I needed. I brought my friends to the dining room for meals and I sat around and talked to people. But it was just too depressing. Everyone was too old." So Gordon returned to his apartment, happy he'd given himself an escape hatch.

The Way We Move Makes a Difference

The way in which we relocate or downsize, including how we separate ourselves from our things, can make a difference to our degree of pain and suffering. In his book *Elderburbia*, Philip Stafford concludes that the loss of one's possessions is "mitigated significantly if the owner is able to exert some control over where things go." He describes the systematic way Anna Simpson distributed family heirlooms when she moved into the residential wing of a long-term care facility. To give herself enough time to carefully distribute her furnishings, she continued to pay rent on her apartment for three months after her move. In this way she was able to identify younger heirs who could be trusted to keep things in the family. Stafford contrasts Anna's experience with what happens to others. "For some residents the luxury of time in these circumstances is limited, as long-distance family members may sweep into town for a few days to get this done all at once and get back to their own lives. The process must feel more violent when it happens that way."[2]

When Kathy and her husband downsized to the condo from their large home she allowed herself months to carefully "de-accession," as she called it. "When my mother-in-law died we had inherited things that were from her grandparents—oak chairs, silver spoons, sentimental quasi-valuable objects. I looked up our wills and saw who was supposed to inherit these things when we died, and I parcelled them out then and there to our children and nieces and nephews. I took great pleasure in both the parcelling out and in seeing these things in their homes when I went to visit. If this had happened after my death, I would have been deprived of the pleasure of the face-to-face gifting. Then there were the things I was thrilled to get rid of—like my dining room set. Our children expressed an interest in some of our art objects, others we donated. After we'd gifted everything we could, we hired a company to run a contents sale and whatever didn't sell they carted away. It was like after a death, but in my case I was being reborn."

One of the most consistent tips from people who've downsized or relocated is to hire help, and the marketplace offers service providers for all aspects of the process. Many people told me they did not want to burden their children with the job, and the advantage of professionals is their specialized knowledge. And, because they've seen it all before, professionals are not easily shocked. Aileen is 74 and has a business helping people downsize from their family home. "I help my clients edit," she explains. "It is wrenching for them to part with their stuff. They're too emotionally involved and need a reality check. The good thing about the exercise is that it helps them to stretch. They've always done the same things the same way and say things like 'our houses are always yellow.' So it lets them shake things up a bit."

At age 82, Marjorie downsized from her home into a condo. Because she hired help, including a professional with Aileen's skills, she found the process to be relatively painless. "I hired a decorator to handle all the modifications in the condo," Marjorie says, "including having a bookcase built, all the window coverings made, recovering the furniture, putting in the closet organizers, adding hardware in the bathroom, et cetera. I got tons of help with packing and unpacking, including someone to help me throw out all the things in the basement and figure out what was going to whom. Then, when we moved in, people helped us unpack everything, including taking the books out of the boxes and putting them into the bookshelf. Every time I needed help, I hired it, which is why everything went very smoothly. Our only problem arose when my husband, who's 84, couldn't manage to sort through his two thousand books. When I told him he had to go through them and figure out which ones he wanted to keep, he replied, 'That's simple. I'll figure out what I want.' So he spent twenty minutes one time and managed to put together a small pile of books, and he never did it again. So because he refused to get rid of them and we don't have room for them all, his books are in storage. That is one regret—we'd both be happier if we had the books he wanted to keep here with us."

If your budget won't allow you to hire help, ask for it. And if you are uncomfortable asking for a handout, or a hand up, do a swap and barter your skills for their services. You'll find some useful downsizing tips in videos by Jane Green on the website www.letssharehousing.com. Topics include starting the sorting process, making the emotional decisions, and to consign or not.

Resources Can Help Our Decision Making

There are a number of tools to help clarify where you want to live. The Hartford Company collaborated with MIT AgeLab to develop a priority list that asks people to rate their preferences when it comes to relationships, region, and resources.[3] Richard Florida's book *Who's Your City* has a section devoted to the location needs and priorities of empty-nesters and retirees, and his website whosyourcity.com has a "place finder" to help people compare where they currently live with their relocation options. Location Scout[4] is an online tool that asks you to rate the importance of such factors as climate, housing options, employment opportunities, cost of living, availability of arts, culture, and recreation, as well as access to transportation, health services, continuing care, and educational opportunities. Our responses are used to identify cities in the US that most closely match our preferences. Although locations in Canada aren't included, going through the thought process is a useful exercise.

The World Health Organization has developed a *Checklist of Essential Features of Age-friendly Cities* based on consultations with older adults conducted in 33 cities in 22 countries. The checklist is designed as a tool to assess the features of a city environment for supporting healthy aging needs. You could use the resource to assess the suitability of your current city/neighbourhood for supporting aging in place or to evaluate the features of a new community. The free tool can be downloaded from WHO's website.[5]

The value of tools such as these is to get you thinking about your future and to provide a starting point for discussion with others who may be involved in the decision. As this next story illustrates, if we don't start talking about our dreams, it's easy to make some false assumptions.

A couple in their sixties, let's call them George and Martha, were close to retirement. George was busying himself with planning a major renovation to their cottage in Muskoka with thoughts that they would sell their city home and relocate to the land of lakes where they would live out their days surrounded by the lapping of the water and the call of the loon. Martha was just as keenly moving in another direction—organizing a life of engagement and activity in the city and looking around for a condo in the heart of the action where they would live out their days strolling to movies, art galleries, and restaurants. Then the day came when they spoke out loud about their very different visions. The person who told me the story said this moment came after they both read *You Could Live a Long Time: Are You Ready?* Evidently, they both expressed utter astonishment that they were on such different pages and the exchange went something like this. George: "Why didn't you realize when I started planning the cottage renovation that I was turning it into our retirement home?" Martha: "I just thought you wanted a bigger cottage for us to use for the next few years." George: "But that's where I want to retire." Martha: "Well that's fine, but you'll be doing it without me." According to my informant, George scrapped the plans and was relieved he hadn't gotten deeper into the renovations. Now they're talking together to plan something that will work for both of them.

If you live in a rural or remote community and want to make it more age-friendly, the report *Age-Friendly Rural and Remote Communities: A Guide* identifies common barriers with the goal of fostering dialogue and action to support change. For example, when it comes to outdoor spaces, barriers include a lack of sidewalks, or continuous sidewalks, and the dangers of walking or using a scooter on busy streets and highways. Even where sidewalks are common, participants were concerned with their state of disrepair and the lack of maintenance of walking trails. Sufficient washrooms and rest areas (especially benches) would make outdoor areas more usable by seniors. A total of 10 communities in eight provinces participated in the research, focusing on the World Health Organization's eight pillars for age-friendly cities referred to earlier in the section on Reasons for Optimism. The report sets out a broad process that communities could follow to address barriers, along with a checklist of age-friendly features that may assist communities to better meet the needs of older adults.[6]

Professionals can be of assistance at all levels of the relocation process, from psychologists to help envision the next stage of our lives, to consultants who specialize in locating retirement homes or long-term care facilities. For the past five years our family has engaged the services of a seniors consultant, who I think of as a geriatric advocate. My parents hired Jane to locate the ideal retirement residence, and when she did and they backed out on moving day, she even managed to get their deposit back. After Mom's medical emergency, it was Jane who helped us negotiate the complicated process of getting them where they are today.

She remains in our employ, advocating and mediating to improve our parents' quality of life. I'm thinking it will soon be time for Jane to start supervising my well-being.

Children Are a Wild Card

Several of the strategies discussed in this book assume supportive offspring, and this is all well and good, when it works. I was told the story of a woman who followed her children to two different cities and relocated each time they moved. When her daughter's employer transferred her yet again, the mother decided to stay put rather than try and adjust to a third new city. Russ tells the story of a friend for whom the tables were reversed. The senior had to relocate to her child's location to help her out in a time of need. "My friend's daughter lost her job," Russ explains, "and the daughter's 17-year-old son, her grandson, was still in school. So the daughter needed some financial support, and fast. My friend sold her house, relocated to their city, moved into their home with them and helped with the mortgage. The daughter finally got a job so the crisis has passed. Although this city would not have been my friend's first choice, she is now reluctant to relocate, and I think she is starting to put down roots."

Betsy doesn't want to be a burden to her children but doesn't think they would have the capacity to help her, anyway. "My children are very supportive," she says, "but they are working full time and raising their children and have no time. And this seems to be the case for most of us. My friend has four children and only one of them is helping her out.

She's only been able to stay in her home because she has a lot of paid support. Fortunately, she was a very social person and her neighbours are always dropping in. And then there is my other friend whose sister just died of Alzheimer's. My friend provided her sister with a lot of support because her two children weren't there for her." As for Betsy, who's 80 years of age, she's decided to move from her condo into a retirement home in two years' time and rely on the paid staff and resources of the facility.

Despite understanding that her children will have full lives, Jennifer fervently hopes they will be a big part of her old age. She is in her sixties, and still living with her husband in the family home. She knows she won't be able to stay in the house when she can no longer climb the stairs, but her dream would be to continue to live in close proximity to her family. "I want to live around people of all ages," she says, "not just all old people like me. Right now I have my husband with me so I don't need to be with people all the time, but I don't know how I would be if I lost him. I don't want to be a burden on my kids and I don't want to be dependent on them, but I do hope they will be there for me. I don't want to just count on friends. When I told my family I would rather age with them around me, they didn't shudder."

Gwen is counting on her daughter to be a help in her old age and had a chance to test out her theory when she broke her hip a few years ago. "After I broke my hip I made arrangements to go into a home that I'd visited a number of times," she says. "It turned out they didn't admit people on weekends and I'd have to wear a mask and couldn't eat my meals with the residents. It sounded like jail. Luckily, my daughter was living in an apartment building with an elevator and she had a spare bedroom. So I stayed there. I know my daughter will be there for me. She'll come around and cut my toenails (which she already does) and wipe my bottom if she has to. But that's only if she still lives nearby."

A factor to consider if you're hoping to engage your children in your care, or at least have them visit you from time to time, is how much it will cost them to make the trip and whether they will be able to afford the expense. Russ has seen the impact on his friends. "My friend was considering a move," Russ recounts, "and his son told him that if he moved away, he'd never get to see him. The travel costs would be too expensive. This is a big issue, especially if you have grandchildren. Similarly, a friend in my condo loves the view—we have the best view in the area—but he's moving to a bigger place to accommodate his visiting family. He told me he's doing this because 'family comes before the view.'" Although Russ doesn't have children, he likes to have visits from his niece and nephew who live in another city. Here's his solution: "I help with the travel costs and tell them it's a loan with no interest and no payment date," he says.

Even if your children are involved in your care, you may not like the outcome. When Debbie was younger she worked on issues of the elderly for the government and was convinced about the value of the philosophy of "the minimum necessary intervention." "You don't want people's independence taken away," she says. "Yet you want them to receive what they need to thrive. And this is always shifting." It has been Debbie's experience that the involvement of children doesn't always help their aging parents. "The children say, 'I want you to do this or that for my mother and/or father,'" Debbie explains, "and they end up taking away some of the responsibilities that make their parents feel good about themselves." And then there is the senior who confessed to me her worst nightmare—that her needy, messy daughter would move in with her.

You May Not Find What You Need

After reading about some of the creative housing options and community services being developed elsewhere, you may have concluded that what you need doesn't exist where you live. As you'll read below, this is the case for Adele and Aileen. Both of them live in small towns that have no current potential to support their desire to stay put and age in place. Despite their longing to stay where they are, both of them will have to relocate unless things change.

Adele is in her sixties and has been living in the same small town for 25 years. She would love to end her days there but unless new facilities are built this won't be possible. As a first step she is prepared to downsize, but there are not many options. And if she really needs care there are even fewer choices. Her 87-year-old mother had been living in a nearby retirement home, but once she started losing mobility and vision she was no longer able to meet the residence requirement of walking unassisted to meals. "We had to look in surrounding communities for options for her," Adele explains, "but the closer nursing homes were so small she'd have to be housed with the dementia patients. This was totally unacceptable because there's nothing wrong with her brain. We've found a home that's quite a distance from me but near enough to other family members that someone can visit her once a week. My mother was a nurse and she knows what's going on and this is not what any of us wanted. What's awful about this system is you get ripped away from your community." Adele has bursitis and, for now, has been able to stay in her home by paying for help with household maintenance. "As for the future," she says, "health is the wild card. What would change everything is if I became dependent in some way."

Aileen is 74 and, like Adele, realizes she will have to move away from her town because of the lack of downsizing options. It had been her intention to buy a townhouse in a new development but the project was rejected by the community. "I was counting on that as my retirement plan," she explains. "I have way more house than I need. I only use about half the space, and I'm not sure how much longer I'll be able to make it up the steps. By not planning ahead for the needs of the people who want to downsize and stay here, this community is being very short-sighted. They want to bring development to a standstill. I love being in my home but so much depends on my health. I live alone and my cleaning lady is in her fifties and I'm older than her mother. She says she worries about coming in one day and finding me dead."

The situation in which Adele and Aileen find themselves could be true for many of us. And it would be very difficult for them, or for any of us, to change these circumstances on their own. It will take collective action to ensure a future of possibilities in our community—not just for ourselves, but for others.

Keep Planning in the Face of Laughter

As Woody Allen said, "If you want to make God laugh, tell him about your plans." Since you never know what life is going to throw at you, what's the point of planning for the future? And since old age often goes on for so long now, opportunities for the unpredictable are legion. As Gwen says, "One of the challenges of old age is that the crises are so hard to predict. You crash all of a sudden." Gwen is 70 and was talking, literally and figuratively, about the hip she had broken recently. She worked part time in a doctor's office and has seen many examples of what she speaks. In addition to medical challenges, countless unexpected developments, both positive and negative, derail the best-laid plans. You've read about many in this book. The death of someone who was integral to your future thinking may force you to change course, you may meet someone late in life and your joint path may take you in a new direction, the birth of a grandchild or the need to assist ailing loved ones may prompt a move, or unexpected work opportunities may open new horizons. And then there are the catastrophes imposed by natural and political disasters. It's easy to justify going with the flow. But the stories you'll read next about Sally and Brian provide powerful counter-arguments.

When I first met Sally, she and her husband, Hal, were in their mid-seventies. Hal was still working three days a week, Sally was busy with volunteer activities, and they were living in the large family home where they had raised their children. They were heading to France that summer for a month and had rented a villa where family members would visit for varying periods of time. That was five years ago, and all was right with the world. Shortly after, Sally fell terribly ill. "It all started when I passed out at the hairdressers," she said, "and I ended up requiring surgery and spending three weeks in the hospital. It was a lengthy illness and I was just getting over it when Hal and I decided to go to New York City to celebrate our anniversary. It was a beautiful warm June day and we walked in the park, had a wonderful dinner, and saw a terrific play. Then at 3 a.m., Hal felt ill and I got him to the hospital where he died of a massive heart attack. I couldn't feel anything—I couldn't cry or laugh. I did things but it was totally on rote. People said that I was so brave, but I was numb. It's only just now— over four years later—that I'm starting to process things." Sally's life changed overnight. She could no longer afford to live in her house and sold it immediately. Fortunately, her sister and brother-in-law were able to find her an apartment in their building, located in the same city and a ready-made community. "All my friends are nearby and we do regular activities together," Sally says. "Some of these routines we've kept up for the past 10 to 12 years." Even if her health deteriorates, Sally's goal is to remain in her apartment and tap into whatever community support she needs. Thinking back to the conversation we had about aging five years ago, Sally says, "I can't believe how sunny I was about it all then. I sounded like a regular Pollyanna!" But I reminded her that she had given me two tips about getting old that now seem very prescient. "Expect the unexpected," she had said. And "If you have an illness, use whatever resources are necessary."

If you've read Joan Didion's book *The Year of Magical Thinking*, you will notice the parallels between Sally's experience and Didion's account of her husband's fatal cardiac arrest while sitting across from her at dinner. As Didion says, "Life changes in the instant. The ordinary instant."[7] Since we don't know what fate has in store for us, some people would cite Sally's and Didion's experiences as proof that planning ahead, including for your future housing needs, is a futile exercise. And since Sally seemed to weather the storm well, people could use her story as a rationale for inaction until the crisis hits. Sally stayed in her home as long as she could, and when it became a necessity, she relocated to suitable accommodation. But let's look at what Sally had going for her when her husband died. She had nurtured an extensive network of family and friends that leapt in post-crisis. Her sister and brother-in-law found her an apartment, and her nephews, granddaughters, and long-standing friends were a great source of strength and assistance. As well, Sally had developed a well-honed resourcefulness and she didn't hesitate to ask for help. When she realized she was going though a depression after Hal's death, she arranged for sessions with a psychologist and a psychiatrist. Also, there were things she had done decades earlier to make her community senior-friendly that are paying off today. When Sally was in her forties, she spent a number of years setting up the first free-standing seniors centre in her area. Her priority was developing the right programming, because she saw it as the most important component of the centre. "I felt the programming had to be something that would appeal to me when I was older and had more leisure time," she says. "Decades later, every one of the programs that we put in place is still there, including a speakers' program where we scheduled talks by professors, and a very big music program including a choir, orchestra, and bell ringing." The staff at the seniors centre has recently asked her to reconnect with them. So it would be inaccurate to say that Sally did not plan ahead for her current life at age 82. Instead, she has been as diligent as a canoeist preparing for a trip down a whitewater river. For decades she's been practising her strokes and building up her strength and making sure her pack contains what she may need. Once she hit the river she had to go with the flow, but she was well equipped to handle the rapids.

Brian's story is another example of the importance of packing well for an unknowable journey. Brian prides himself on his strategy of planning ahead in 10-year increments, envisioning his ideal situation. When he was in his early sixties he started acquiring the land and drawing up the plans for a dream retirement home perched on a hillside with a spectacular view. He moved in when he was in his early seventies. It was paradise on earth—for awhile. "I had thought this would be my final resting place," Brian says, "and they would plant my ashes under the cedar tree. I hadn't realized that the splendid isolation would come at a cost. I began to miss the intellectual stimulation, and started to feel a certain emptiness. I realized I couldn't keep my brain alive without projects and they were hard to find there. Then there were the practical problems—I was miles from a hospital, an airport, and my social community."

Brian had already decided he was going to give up his beautiful home and move closer to friends and medical services when fate intervened. It took the form of a hurricane. "I had been trying to figure a way out and then I watched my house slide down the hill," he says. "Be careful what you wish for." Although he had received the push he wanted, it came at a cost. He was ready to abandon the property and relocate closer to friends and services but he was not fully compensated for his losses. So he would have to make the move and acquire land and rebuild without adequate funds. This is where Brian's lifetime of preparation paid off. "I had several things going for me," Brian says. "I have the ability to be very positive. And I have a huge support system that includes a lot of young people. I was able to use my longtime connections to find the land, and the house was built by my young friends, who scrounged the material and volunteered their time. I could not have survived this without these young people and their affection and caring." But this extraordinary support system of Brian's did not just miraculously appear. For years, Brian has been a father figure and mentor to these young men and women, and his crisis gave them an opportunity to give back.

Like Sally, Brian had been preparing for years for this outcome. "Throughout my life, once I knew what I wanted to do, I would try and get as many people around to help me," Brian explains. "I always assemble a support system. And, in the same way, I try and help others. I am curious and always expanding my network of interconnection. Part of this is my ability to connect with people regardless of their station in life. My philosophy has always been to treat people as equals, regardless of their social standing. I have always had incredible support from young people and I think it's because I have an ability to recognize their latent talent."

We can learn from Brian and Sally. Even without knowing the game plan, we would be wise to build our readiness and steel ourselves to the sounds of God's mirth.

We Make Our Own Bed

When I asked the role models in *You Could Love a Long Time: Are You Ready?* for their advice on what I should be doing now to live well at their advanced years, they emphasized working on my self-knowledge and my self-acceptance, sustaining my emotional circle, having a work plan rather than a retirement plan, developing my civic engagement and my sense of humour, and paying attention to my heart and my soul. As we focus on the details of our living space, it is important that we not neglect these things. They will help us feel at home, wherever we are.

The stories in this book are about many people who got this balance right. Theirs are tales of personal growth and renewal, and joy at being at home. There's Henry strolling with Jean in the gardens of Silver Sage Village, greeting the fellow residents who are supporting him in Jean's dementia care. There's 101-year-old Gordon packing up to leave the well-appointed retirement home because the residents are too old. He describes himself as a romantic and his 100th birthday party featured tango dancers. So I'm thinking he didn't find the facility to be *gezellig*. Then there's Irma's role model—a 90-year-old friend who lives alone, despite being blind. "She is a tremendous flirt," Irma says with admiration. "She has a guy who takes her everywhere. People come to do her hair. She's managing it so well. She has made a pact to die at the same time as her best friend but they can't get it together because one or the other always has something booked that interferes with the plan." There's Ned, who's orchestrating life in his unconventional rooming housing with an emphasis on conviviality and celebration. And then there is my father. Ever since he and my mother were safely housed, and despite his memory and mobility challenges, Dad has grabbed the best of what remains of his life. His room is festooned with photos of those times he's managed, with the help of his family, to go AWOL from the long-term care facility. In one photo, he's at the 2010 Vancouver Olympics, nearby is a close-up of him being kissed by a dolphin in a pool in Cuba. There he is, in another, in the cockpit of a speeding boat rounding La Ronde off Old Montreal, and that's him seated at a sumptuously laden table at the Officers' Mess looking dashing in a be-medalled tuxedo.

So that's probably the most important thing I've learned from these veterans of life. Once I've done everything I can to get my housing right and I've made my bed, I'll need to lie in it. And I may as well do it in style.

Preparing My Defence

THE LONG-TERM care facility where my parents now reside is one of the best in the country and they are lucky to be there. We'll never know where they might be today had they been able to seize their future. But we can say with certainty that their journey would have been less painful—for their family and friends, but particularly for them. I said it was lucky that my parents ended up in their excellent care facility, but luck really had very little to do with it. Their emotional circle worked tirelessly for two years to get them to the place where they are today— a place where people care both for them and about them. This outpouring of care for my parents is not surprising. All their lives, they wrapped their children in boundless love and support, and were ferociously loyal to family and generous to friends. So when they needed help, there was a deep well of love and gratitude from which to draw.

My parents are far from alone in inspiring this kind of support. The stories in this book are filled with similar examples, along with much more extravagant displays. For four years, Simon coordinated a care team that allowed his mother to live in her own home until her death. Stephanie and her husband built a new home to include a suite for Stephanie's mother when she found it difficult to live alone. Noreen's brother bought a house large enough to accommodate both his mother as well as her caregiver, and he coordinates her round-the-clock care. After Ian had a stroke, his care team, which included his legal advisors, family, his former secretary, and several friends, wrapped up his business, sold his house, coordinated his medical care, and moved him to the residence of his choice.

These are all examples of that Plan B to which I alluded earlier. As you may have surmised, the backup plan consists of enlisting our emotional circle to care for us and, most importantly, care about us. That circle will include our friends and family, as well as paid caregivers and strategic thinkers like our geriatric advocate, Jane. For even if we do everything in our power to house ourselves for the future, we'll want their help. So we need to be nurturing that circle now, because we're going to need it.

Although I wrote this book for we aging folks, I had my daughters and all the younger generations in mind. If we don't figure out how to care for ourselves in our old age, they'll be in trouble right alongside us. Our daughters claim that their father and I share many of my parents' character traits, and they won't be surprised to see us repeating their history and stubbornly staying in a house no longer suitable for us. But I'm going to do my best to prove them wrong. I intend to use what I've learned from writing this book to try and stay independent, engaged, and living in the home of my choosing, right to the end. My hope is that when we need to enact Plan B and call upon them, our demands will be minimal.

But I confess that what really worries me is the judgment of my own court of opinion. In her essay "On Keeping a Notebook," Joan Didion encourages us to stay in touch with our previous selves. "I think we are well advised to keep on nodding terms with the people we used to be," she writes, "whether we find them attractive company or not. Otherwise they turn up unannounced and surprise us, come hammering on the mind's door at 4 a.m. of a bad night and demand to know who deserted them, who betrayed them, who is going to make amends."[1] When I think of the self that I will be in my old age, I am reminded of Didion's warning. I fear that the senior me might receive that early morning visitor who will look around at my surroundings and demand an accounting. I'll ask myself, "How did you let this happen?"

My mother has these visitations. Although she floats in and out of the here and now, from time to time there is an abrupt surfacing. One of those times she looked me straight in the eye and said, "I never knew it would be like this." Unlike my mother, I won't be able to make that claim. I do have a pretty good sense of the possible outcomes. So I am preparing my defence. This book, and my plan to act on its findings, will comprise my evidence that, regardless of the success of the outcome, I made a genuine effort to realize the future I thought I wanted.

Notes

INTRODUCTION

1. Witold Rybczynski, *Home: A Short History of an Idea* (New York: Penguin Books, 1986), 63. Rybczynski notes that German, Danish, Swedish, Icelandic, Dutch, and English all have similar sounding words for *home* derived from the Old Norse *heima*.

THE HARD FACTS

1. *The Safe Living Guide—A guide to home safety for seniors*. (Ottawa, ON: Public Health Agency of Canada, 2011), 6. Available at http://www.phac-aspc.gc.ca/seniors-aines/publications/public/injury-blessure/safelive-securite/pdfs/safelive-securite-eng.pdf.

2. S. Vandentorren, P. Bretin., A. Zeghnoun, et al. "August 2003 heat wave in France: risk factors for death of elderly people living at home," *Eur J Public Health* 2006, 16: 583–91.

3. http://www.fin.gov.on.ca/en/budget/ontariobudgets/2012/ch1.html.

4. The study, *Projecting the Adequacy of Canadians' Retirement Incomes: Current Prospects and Possible Reform Options*, can be downloaded from the Institute's website at www.irpp.org.

5. The statistics cited in the report are from *Statistics Canada: A Gender-based Statistical Report*, 5th edition, 2006. "Poor" means an income after tax below Statistics Canada's low-income cut-off (LICO). For 2006, the after-tax LICO was $17,568 for a one-person household living in a city of over half a million. About two of every five women aged 65 and over live alone, more than twice the average for men. http://www.statcan.gc.ca/pub/75f0002m/75f0002m2008004-eng.pdf.

6. The co-op now operates separately from OWN, under the Co-operative Corporations Act.

7. For additional information about OWN's activities, and to obtain a copy of the report from the 2009 public forum, visit their website at http://olderwomensnetwork.org.

8. The definition of disability used in the report is based on the World Health Organization's framework of disability, provided by the International Classification of Functioning (ICF). This framework defines disability as "impairment, activity limitation or participation restriction that is the result of the interaction between contextual factors (personal and environmental) and health conditions." http://www.hrsdc.gc.ca/eng/disability_issues/reports/fdr/2011/page05.shtml.

9. D.B. Carr, K.L. Flood, K. Steger-May, K.B. Schechtman, and E.F. Binder, "Characteristics of Frail Older Adult Drivers," *Journal of the American Geriatrics Society*, 54: 1125–29.

10. Ezra Hauer, "In defence of older drivers," *CMAJ*, April 3, 2012, 184: E305–E306.

11. Diana Athill, *Somewhere Towards the End* (New York: W.W. Norton and Company, Inc., 2009), 107.

12. Mickey Meece, "Car-Pooling Makes a Surge on Apps and Social Media," *New York Times*, July 4, 2012.

REASONS FOR OPTIMISM

1. A copy of the report can be downloaded from http://www.nyc.gov/html/dfta/html/age/age-friendly.shtml.

2. http://www.silive.com/westshore/index.ssf/2011/10/sea_view_jcc_to_house_a_city_i.html.

3. http://www.mountsinai.org/patient-care/service-areas/geriatrics-and-aging/news/mount-sinai-opens-new-york-citys-first-emergency-room-for-geriatric-patients.

4. Gary Chalk, "They are the masters of aging," *Brantford Expositor*, September 6, 2011 (http://www.brantfordexpositor.ca/ArticleDisplay.aspx?e=3285977&archive=true). For copies of the Master Aging Plan and the Implementation Action Plan see the city of Brantford's website, http://www.brantford.ca/govt/projects/Pages/MasterAgingPlan.aspx.

5. The World Health Organization's model for age-friendly cities has eight pillars. Along with housing, the other pillars are outdoor spaces and buildings, transportation, social participation, respect and social inclusion, civic participation and employment, communication and information, and community support and health services. Details can be found in their report *Global Age-friendly Cities: A Guide* (2007), which can be downloaded at http://www.who.int/ageing/publications/Global_age_friendly_cities_Guide_English.pdf.

6. Nora Ephron, *I Remember Nothing* (New York: Random House, 2010), 11.

7. Natasha Singer, "The Fountain of Old Age," *New York Times*, Feb. 6, 2011.

8. Allan S. Teel, *Alone and Invisible No More: How Grassroots Community Action and 21st Century Technologies Can Empower Elders to Stay in Their Homes and Lead Healthier, Happier Lives* (White River Junction VT: Chelsea Green Publishing, 2011), 86.

9. Ibid., xiii.

WHAT WE NEED FROM OUR HOME

1. J.B. James, E. Besen, C. Matz-Costa, and M. Pitt-Catsouphes, *Just do it? . . . maybe not! Insights on activity in later life from the Life & Times in an Aging Society Study* (Chestnut Hill, MA: Sloan Center on Aging & Work, Boston College, 2012).

2. http://www.hrsdc.gc.ca/eng/success_stories/seniors/25/index.shtml.

3. For more details see http://www.elliotlake.com/retire/.

4. S. Vandentorren, P. Bretin, A. Zeghnoun, et al., "August 2003 heat wave in France: risk factors for death of elderly people living at home," *Eur J Public Health* 2006, 16: 583–91.

5. Karene Brooker, "Effects of loneliness mimic aging process" in *Psychology and Psychiatry*, May 1, 2012, as reported in *Psychology and Aging* (27:1). http://medicalxpress.com/news/2012-05-effects-loneliness-mimic-aging.html.

6. Wid Chapman and Jeffrey P. Rosenfeld, *Unassisted Living: Ageless Homes for Later Life* (New York: The Monacelli Press, 2011), 173.

7. Jane Jacobs, *The Death and Life of Great American Cities* (New York: Vintage Books, 1992), 35.

8. Philip B. Stafford, *Elderburbia: Aging with a Sense of Place in America* (Santa Barbara, CA: ABC-CLIO, LLC, 2009), 23.

9. The ENABLE-AGE Project conducted home interviews with 1,918 people aged 75 to 89 years living alone in their own homes in Swedish, German, British, Hungarian, and Latvian urban areas. Andrew Sixsmith, Carita Nygren, Doerte Naumann, Frank Oswald, Hans-Werner Wahl, Zsuzsa Szeman, Signe Tomsone, Melany Ball, Robert Ingram, ENABLE-AGE Policy Recommendations http://www.enableage.arb.lu.se/documents/ENABLE-AGE%20Policy%20recommendations.pdf.

10. The *Age Friendly Checklist Results 2011* is found here: http://www.centretownchc.org/media/96824/assess_your_park___age_friendly_checklist.pdf. The *Age Friendly Park Checklist* is found here: http://www.centretownchc.org/media/82158/shpc_agefriendly_park_checklistfinal.pdf.

11. Elizabeth Bream, "My unexpected third act," *Globe and Mail*, March 28, 2012.

12. Gerry Hyman, "Women entitled to use lobby for chats," *Toronto Star*, March 24, 2012.

13. For more information see http://www.yarrowecovillage.ca.

14. http://www.huffingtonpost.com/2011/02/15/boom-retirement-community_n_823535.html#s240578&title=J_Mayer_H.

15. John Tagliabue, "Taking on Dementia With the Experiences of Normal Life," *New York Times*, April 24, 2012.

16. For more information see their website at http://www.wolfcreeklodge.org/.

MODIFYING OUR HOME

1. F. Oswald, H.-W. Wahl, O. Schilling, C. Nygren, A. Fänge, A. Sixsmith, Z. Szeman, S. Tomsone, and S. Iwarsson, "Relationships Between Housing and Healthy Aging in Very Old Age," *The Gerontologist* (2007) 47 (1): 96–107.

2. Andrew Sixsmith, Carita Nygren, Doerte Naumann, Frank Oswald, Hans-Werner Wahl, Zsuzsa Szeman, Signe Tomsone, Melany Ball, Robert Ingram, ENABLE-AGE Policy Recommendations (http://www.enableage.arb.lu.se/documents/ENABLE-AGE%20Policy%20recommendations.pdf).

3. The website of the Center for Universal Design at NC State University outlines the principles of universal design. http://www.ncsu.edu/project/design-projects/udi/center-for-universal-design/the-principles-of-universal-design/.

4. *The Safe Living Guide* can be downloaded from http://www.phac-aspc.gc.ca/seniors-aines/publications/public/injury-blessure/safelive-securite/pdfs/safelive-securite-eng.pdf.

5. Available at http://www.cmhc-schl.gc.ca/en/co/maho/adse/masein/.

6. Available at http://www.cmhc-schl.gc.ca/odpub/pdf/61042.pdf.

7. Available at http://www.cmhc-schl.gc.ca/en/co/renoho/refash/refash_033.cfm#CP_JUMP_158065.

8. These publications can be downloaded from their website at http://hartfordauto.thehartford.com/Safe-Driving/Expertise-On-Getting-Older/Publications-And-Resources/.

9. Chapman and Rosenfeld, *Unassisted Living*, 9.

10. For details see http://www.gov.ns.ca/coms/housing/seniors/Seniors-Independence.html.

11. For details, visit the Saskatchewan Housing Corporation website at www.socialservices.gov.sk.ca/housing.

12. For details, see CMHC's website at www.cmhc.ca.

13. For example, in Toronto, at the time of writing, if you have more than four unrelated people living together in your home you are operating a rooming house. You will require a licence and need to meet certain standards, including more restrictive fire code regulations.

COMMUNITY SUPPORT

1. F. Oswald, H.-W. Wahl, O. Schilling, C. Nygren, A. Fänge, J. Sixsmith, A. Szeman, S. Tomsone, and S. Iwarsson, "Relationships Between Housing and Healthy Aging in Very Old Age," *The Gerontologist* (2007) 47 (1): 96–107.

2. The website of the Canadian Home Care Association (www.cdnhomec are.ca), which has a national membership of over 400 homecare organizations, provides resources to help you understand how the system works in your area.

3. SPRINT is one of countless community organizations across the country offering services to the elderly. Many of them receive some government funding, and each province and territory has resources to help you locate them. For example, see the Ontario Community Support Association, which represents not-for-profit community agencies, provides resources to people looking for a home and community support provider at http://homeandcommunitysupport.ca. The Ontario Ministry of Health and Long-Term Care provides advice on selecting home, community, and residential care services for seniors at http://www.health.gov.on.ca/en/public/programs/ltc/19_provider.aspx.

4. http://www.beaconhillvillage.org/content.aspx?page_id=22&club_id=332658&module_id=77064.

5. http://www.darts1.org/news/dhs-funding-supports-darts-homemak-ing-and-outdoor-chore-services.

6. Stafford, *Elderburbia*, 134.

7. Teel, *Alone and Invisible No More*, xiii.

HOMESHARING

1. Deborah E. Altus, R. Mark Mathews, "Examining Satisfaction of Older Home Owners with Intergenerational Homesharing," *Journal of Clinical Geropsychology* Volume 6, Number 2, 2000-04-01.

2. Personal correspondence, May 31, 2012, and September 19, 2012.

3. Available at http://www.caring.com/articles/arranging-home-share.

4. Available at http://www.cmhc-schl.gc.ca/en/co/reho/index.cfm.

5. Ron Lieber, "Airbnb's Lodging Gets Tested, Yielding a Mixed Bag," *New York Times*, Nov. 12, 2011.

SHARING SPACE WITH CHILDREN

1. Available at http://www.pahousingchoices.org/uploads/Self-Help-Guide-Shared-Hsg0001.pdf.

2. For more information see http://www.gov.ns.ca/coms/housing/seniors/ParentApartmentProgram.html.

3. Ted Fishman, *Shock of Gray* (New York: Scribner, 2010), 148.

4. Go to http://www.cmhc-schl.gc.ca/odpub/pdf/66642.pdf. Your municipality may have planning or zoning regulations governing garden suites. These regulations can set restrictions, such as distance from the permanent house, parking requirements, how long a garden suite can stay on a lot, and the appearance of the garden suite. See the CMHC Fact Sheet on Garden Suites at http://www.cmhc-schl.gc.ca/en/co/renoho/refash/refash_026.cfm.

5. Linda Baker, "New co-housing community backs market trends," http://www.oregonbusiness.com/linda/7370-co-housing-community-bucks-market-trends-#ixzz1vFnJjl1i.

6. P.J. Bremier, "Under the Living Roof," *Marin Magazine*, March 2009 (http://www.marinmagazine.com/Marin-Magazine/March-2009/Under-the-Living-Roof/).

SHARING SPACE WITH OTHER FAMILY

1. Martin Amis, *Experience* (Hyperion: New York, 2000), 286, 306, 311, 312.

DOWNSIZING

1. The guide can be downloaded from their website at http://www.cmhc-schl.gc.ca/odpub/pdf/63100.pdf.

2. Susan Seliger, "In the Backyard, Grandma's New Apartment," *New York Times*, May 1, 2012. For more information see http://medcottage.com.

COHOUSING

1. Jim Leach, "Senior Cohousing—A Great Place for Baby Boomers To Live Mindfully: My Observations and Experience at Silver Sage Village, Senior Cohousing," October 26, 2009, http://whdc.com/documents/SeniorCohousingmyexperience.pdf.

2. Stafford, *Elderburbia*, 139.

3. Eliza Meggs, "Cohousing: A New Option for Seniors," *Wholife*, Volume 16, Issue 2, July/August 2010.

4. Charles Durrett, *The Senior Cohousing Handbook* (Gabriola Island, BC: New Society Publishers, 2nd edition, 2009), 120.

5. Ibid., 199.

6. Peter Block, *Community: The Structure of Belonging* (San Francisco: Bar-rett-Koehler Publishers, Inc., 2009), 185.

SENIORS HOUSING

1. See http://www.lifelease.ca/projects/St%20Vital%20Knights%20Villa/ST%20VITAL%20VILLA.html.

2. Arielle Godbout, "Growing intergenerational connections," *Winnipeg Free Press*, September 7, 2011. http://www.winnipegfreepress.com/our-com-munities/lance/Growing-intergenerational-connections-129327103. html.

3. See http://www.lifelease.ca/projects/Winnipeg%20River/WINNIPEG %20RIVER%20MANOR.html.

4. "Alternate Tenure Arrangements," Socio-Economic Series, Issue 65, CMHC Fact Sheet. http://publications.gc.ca/collections/Collection/NH18-23-65E.pdf.

5. The report can be downloaded at https://www03.cmhc-schl.gc.ca/cata-log/productDetail.cfm?cat=126&itm=3&lang=en&fr=1343160370751.

6. The report can be downloaded at http://www.communitylivingbc.ca/wp-content/uploads/Financing-Seniors-Equity-Final-Report-08.pdf.

RELIGIOUS/ETHNOCULTURAL/SPIRITUAL COMMUNITIES

1. For more information see www.taubekoretcampus.org.

2. David Hayes, "Senior home thinks 'outside the box,'" *Toronto Star*, Jan-uary 28, 2012.

3. Catey Hill, "Retire Here, Not There: Ohio," *SmartMoney*, June 17, 2012. http://www.smartmoney.com/retirement/planning/retire-here-not-there-ohio-1339536992810/.

4. Letter to the Editor, "Re: Getting On With Life After a Partner Dies," *New York Times*, June 22, 2010. For more information on Kendal communities see http://www.kendal.org/.

5. Dakshana Bascaramurty, "Ethnic-focused nursing homes put a Canadian face on filial piety," *Globe and Mail*, January 27, 2012.

6. Linda Grant, *Remind Me Who I Am, Again* (London: Granata, 1998), 176.

7. Bascaramurty, "Ethnic-focused nursing homes put a Canadian face on filial piety."

8. David Hayes, "Aging in place is simple at Hesperus Village," *Toronto Star*, January 14, 2012.

SUPPORTIVE HOUSING

1. "French feminists rethink 'old-age,'" Expatica.com, January 30, 2012. http://www.expatica.com/fr/news/news_focus/French-feminists-rethink-oldage-_196128.html?ppager=0.

2. For more information, see their website at www.abbeyfieldsaanichpeninsula.org.

3. For more information, see http://www.niagararegion.ca/living/seniors/programs/supportive-housing.aspx.

4. "A unique co-op," November 8, 2008, on thestar.com at http://www.thestar.com/atkinsonseries/article/532232--a-unique-co-op#comments.

5. For more information visit http://www.dixonhall.org/our-services/senior-programs/supportive-housing/.

6. For more information see the organization's website at www.circleofcare.com.

7. The Health Transition Fund Final Report for Project BC122, March 30, 2000, can be downloaded at http://www2.itssti.hc-sc.gc.ca/hpb/hcpd/pchcd/projectc.nsf/ExecSum/BC122/$File/BC122.pdf.

CONTINUUM OF CARE

1. Gerald Hodge, *The Geography of Aging: Preparing Communities for the Surge in Seniors* (Montreal and Kingston: McGill-Queen's University Press, 2008), 207. To support independence, Hodge proposes the kinds of policies and programs for housing, transportation, and community support that we are discussing in this book. Seniors can be maintained in their homes through programs such as meals on wheels, volunteer drivers, and/or shopping. Alternative housing can be made available in pedestrian-friendly, transit-accessible locations. Formal support can include home nursing, adult daycare, seniors centres, recreation programs, and transportation services.

2. Ibid., 211.

LESSONS LEARNED

1. F. Oswald, H.-W. Wahl, O. Schilling, C. Nygren, A. Fänge, J. Sixsmith, Z. Szeman, S. Tomsone, and S. Iwarsson, "Relationships Between Housing and Healthy Aging in Very Old Age," *The Gerontologist* (2007) 47 (1): 96–107.

2. Stafford, *Elderburbia*, 4.

3. "Modern Ideas, Modern Living: Taking the Next Step in Home Design and Planning for the Lifestyle You Want," prepared by the Hartford and MIT AgeLab, March 2011, can be downloaded from http://hartfordauto.thehartford.com/UI/Downloads/modernliving.pdf.

4. See http://www.aarp.org/home-garden/livable-communities/location-scout-find-best-place-live/.

5. www.who.int/ageing/publications/Age_friendly_cities_checklist.pdf.

6. The document, prepared for the Federal/Provincial/Territorial Ministers Responsible for Seniors, can be downloaded at http://www.phac-aspc.gc.ca/seniors-aines/publications/public/afc-caa/rural-rurales/index-eng.php.

7. Joan Didion, *The Year of Magical Thinking* (New York: Vintage International, 2007), 3.

PREPARING MY DEFENCE

1. Joan Didion, *Slouching Towards Bethlehem* (New York: First Washington Square Press, 1981), 142.